THE NSE PROPHECY

Assessing the Impact of Elections
on Stock Markets and
Quality of Life

THE NSE PROPHECY

Assessing the Impact of Elections
on Stock Markets and
Quality of Life

CPA WILSON MBUGUA

The author assumes full responsibility for all content of this book

Published by Sahel Publishing Association,
a subsidiary of Sahel Books Inc.
P.O. Box 21232 – 00505
Nairobi, Kenya
Tel: +011-254-715-596-106
For questions and orders log on to:
www.sahelpublishing.net

A Sahel Book
Nairobi. New Delhi. London. Nashville.
Editor: Sam Okello
Interior and cover design by: Hellen Wahonya Okello
Printed in India

To my departed parents Mr. Samuel Ngugi and
Mrs. Flora Nyokabi

Acknowledgements

This book was made possible by a number of people and institutions to whom I am greatly indebted and to whom I would like to express a lot of gratitude.

I am grateful to God for having given me strength to go through the study of stock markets and complete this book. I thank the great team of advisors for continuous guidance and advice they gave during my writing.

I extend special thanks to my wife, Lois Mbugua, for moral support and encouragement during the writing period. To our daughter, Abigail Nyokabi, and sons, David Ngugi, Joseph Wangai and James Chege, thanks for your encouraging smiles. I also appreciate my departed parents for giving me education without which I could not have written this book.

I must also extend my sincere gratitude to my friends who encouraged me during the writing period and to other people who contributed to this book in one way or another. Thank you all.

Finally, my heartfelt appreciation to my publisher, Sahel Publishing Association, and the capable team led by Hon Sam Okello and Madam Hellen Wahonya Okello, for enabling me to realize my dream of being a published author. May my contribution play a role in demystifying the role of stock markets in Africa.

Foreword

If there has ever been a subject matter that has remained shrouded in mystery for the vast majority of people in the world, it is the matter of stock markets. Many of us are clueless how stock markets work and, perhaps, more ominous, is the fact that we don't know and don't understand how stock markets affect ordinary people – he or she who is not a player in the world of stock trading.

In this timely book, *The NSE Prophecy*, CPA Wilson Mbugua delves into the matter of stocks and explains in detail how markets affect us in our daily lives. But, perhaps, the most important contribution of all is the author's desire to weave together three critical elements to the African voter – through the prism of Kenya: the policies of a party, the flagbearer of the party and the quality of life of the voter. In essence, what the author says is that it matters who one votes for.

In reaction to the voted party and personality of the party's flagbearer, the stock market is always a reliable prophesier of future trends in the economy of a nation. This is the reason Wilson sees stock markets as a prophetic tool for policymakers and key stakeholders in the maintenance of a peaceful environment where trade can flourish.

I know of no better scholar – an astute accountant with years of experience as an auditor at PricewaterhouseCoopers, pension fund trustee, and a Financial Analyst for an international development agency – than CPA Wilson Mbugua to have handled this subject matter with credibility. He is a member of the Institute of Certified Public Accountants of Kenya (ICPAK) and Information Systems Auditors and Control Association (ISACA).

His role as a trustee of a pension scheme and council member of the Association of Retirement Benefits Schemes (ARBS)- have exposed him to economic, social and political treads locally and globally that enabled him put this book together. His book couldn't have come at a better time to help voters around the world to understand their role in shaping their destiny through the power of the vote. As his Excellency, the second president of Kenya, Daniel Arap Moi, used to say: *siasa mbaya, maisha mbaya*, meaning bad politics leads to poor quality of life or choices have consequences.

Dr. Nicholas Letting, PhD (UoN), HSC, FCPA (K), MKIM, CPS (K)
Vice-Chancellor Management University of Africa

Contents

List of Figures

List of Abbreviations

AD	Anno Domini
ARBS	Association of Retirement Benefits Schemes
ASEA	African Securities Exchange Association
ATS	Automated Trading System
CBK	Central Bank of Kenya
CDSA	Central Depository Settlement Authority
CMA	Capital Markets Authority
COMESA	Common Market for Eastern and Southern Africa
CPA	Certified Public Accountant
DASS	Delivery And Settlement System
DNA	Deoxyribonucleic Acid
ECOWAS	Economic Community of West African States
ICPAK	Institute of Certified Public Accountants of Kenya

IEBC	Independent Electoral Boundaries Commission
IGAD	Intergovernmental Authority For Development
IFC	International Finance Corporation
IMF	International Monetary Fund
IPO	Initial Public Offer
ISAKA	Information Systems Auditors and Control Association
KADU	Kenya African Democratic Union
KANU	Kenya African National Union
KBC	Kenya Commercial Bank
NARC	National Rainbow Coalition
NASI	NSE All Share Index
NEMU	National Election Monitoring Unit
NSE	Nairobi Securities Exchange
ODM	Orange Democratic Movement
S&P 500 Index	Standard & Poors 500 Index

Glossary

Academic Something educational

Accountability Being answerable for one's actions

African Securities Exchange Association Organization that looks into the interests of Africa's stock market

Agikuyu Kenya's largest ethnic group

Ancestral Land Land inherited from the forefathers

Anno Domini After death

Assassination Elimination of a political opponent through murder

Al Shabaab A terrorist organization operating in the horn of Africa

Autocratic Exhibiting Dictatorial tendencies

Automated Trading System A digitized platform for buying and selling stocks

Bank of England The central bank of England

Bear Market General increase in prices of shares in a stock market

Big Man Syndrome African dictators with a larger than life personality cult built around them

Blueprint A laid down plan for tackling issues raised on a matter of concern

Boko Haram Terrorist organization in Western Africa

Bretton Woods Institutions IMF and World Bank

British Colony A nation or land formerly owned or run by England

Bull Market General decrease in prices of shares in a stock market

Capacity Building Enhancing skill levels for the sake of better performance and productivity

Capital Gains Tax Taxes on the increase in value of assets

Capital Markets Authority The institution in Kenya charged with regulating the raising of long-term capital

Civilian Coup The act of a military to install a civilian of choice into a nation's leadership

Civil Wars Pogroms within a nation occasioned by internal strife

Coalition Government The coming together of two opposing political thoughts to form a government for the sole purpose of uniting a nation

Cohesiveness A state of being in perfect harmony

Colonial A product of a period when colonies existed

Commonwealth A member of the sisterhood of nations that were once British colonies

Conglomerate A company whose reach is cross- border

Congress The House of Representatives in the United States of America

Conservative One with deeply held traditional ideas undisturbed by modern trends

Constitution The supreme law of the land

Continent One of the six land masses surrounded by oceans to make the world

Cronyism Unabashed sycophancy

Debt A state of owing someone or an institution

Democrat A person whose political leanings are center-left

Devolution The act of decentralizing services and governance to the counties

Dictatorship A form of governance devoid of participatory tendencies

Ecclesiocracy A hybrid government where state officials are clergy, but policies are secular

Emerging Capital Markets Young stock markets

Economic Decline Steady scaling back of the building block of growth

Economic Environment The sum of all systems that come together to spur or stagnate growth

Economic Meltdown The Crash of systems that control growth

Election Reaction Effect The stock market's sentiment after an election outcome

Elections Democratically choosing representatives

Environment The prevailing atmosphere around a given place

Federal Reserve The Central Bank of the United States of America

Feel Good Effect A general warmth generated in a nation based on a positive trend in leadership

Firm A legally set up company

Fiscal Discipline The prudent management of financial resources in a nation

Fiscal Policy Systems put in place to guide management of financial resources

Flexibility The ability to adjust quickly to changing circumstances

Foreigners Investors who are not citizens of the nation they have chosen to invest in

Functioning Legislature A law-making body that acts independently of Executive or any other influence

Government A way society is organized to handle its peculiar matters

Horn of Africa In reference to the nations to the far Eastern end of the continent of Africa e.g. Somalia and Djibouti

Humanism A philosophical period when man put himself at the center of the universe, which is how rugged individualism was born

Illiteracy An inability to read or write

Incentive A sweetener designed to goad an investor into committing funds into a market

Industrial Dow Jones A measure of the performance of the stock market in the United States

Infrastructure A set way systems and operations are expected to flow

Independent Judiciary A legal system that acts

outside the influence of the Executive, Legislature or any other influence

Indicator   Signs of trends on a stock market

Institutions   Legally set up bodies tasked to fulfil a certain purpose

Labour   A center left political party in the United Kingdom

Liberal   Progressive in thought

Land Redistribution   A liberal policy of progressives in Kenya to equitably share land as a factor of wealth creation

Market Sentiment   The prevailing feeling on a given period about the future of a market

Mau Mau Uprising   A rebellion staged by Africans in Kenya to rid their land of the white settlers

Milestones   Key measures of progress

Military   A network of forces legally set up to handle arms in the protection of a nation's territorial integrity

Monarchy   A form of government in which sovereignty is embodied in one or several individuals reigning until abdication

Monetary Policy Systems put in place by a central bank to govern management of money

Multiparty Politics   A situation where several legally set up parties are contemplated by the Constitution to be in contention for power

National Healing The prospect of a nation coming together as one

Natural Calamities Occurrences precipitated by nature with harmful effect on human life e.g. earth quakes

Nepotism The act of placing one's own tribesmen in key positions of leadership

Oligarchy   A small group of people having control of a country, organization or institution

One Party Dictatorship A nation governed under one party

Pariah Status Facing international scorn based on ignoble leadership

Parliament A national house where the people's representatives converge to make laws

Party Effect The impact on the stock market of a party that's gained the majority after an election

Performance The ups and downs experienced on a stock market

Police State A repressive autocracy in which the fundamental rights of citizens are ruthlessly fought

Policy Makers People tasked to set systems in place for the guidance of a company

Policy A framework for rules of engagement

Political Environment The stability or lack thereof occasioned by the actions of national leaders

Political Stability Prevailing peace in a nation dependent on the nature of politics at play

Political Upheavals Melt down in the governance in a nation

Post-independence Africa African nations after independence

Poverty Lack of basic human needs

Predictability The ability to reliably forecast the future based on patterns of the past

Progressives Liberals

Promulgation A wholesale shift from an old constitutional dispensation to a new one

Prophecy Prediction of the future

Profitable Opportunities The existence of stocks one may invest in to draw big returns

Publicly-quoted Companies Firms with shares floated on the stock market

Quality of Life The manner people live based on the politics, economics and social circumstances in a nation

Recessionary Period Moments of slow growth in an economy

Repression Using brute force to silence opposition or alternative thought

Republican A conservative in American politics

Residual Claim The entitlement of ordinary shareholders to the profits of a company or proceeds from dissolution of a company

Responsible Executive A presidency that has its ear on the ground on matters affecting citizens

Rightwing Being center-right in political leanings

Rugged Individualism A state in which selfishness is at the core of human operations

Scarce Resources Limited investments assets

Second-half Effect The rise in stock prices after the first half of a presidency

Short-term A limited period of time

Skills A core set of abilities that enable a certain task to be accomplished

Stakeholders Having an interest in a firm's performance

State House The place of residency of a the Kenyan president

Status Quo The desire to leave things in place

Structural adjustment Rethinking and acting in new ways to achieve better results

Stockbrokers Traders or players in a stock market

Stock Market The place publicly traded companies converge to float shares

Systems A network or infrastructure through which a firm accomplishes its goals

Tory Center-right party in UK politics

Terror The act of using extreme violence to communicate

Theocracy A government under the leadership of God

Vetting The act of screening an official for public office

Vibrant Press An independent media

Vision 2030 Kenya's economic blueprint toward achieving the status of an industrialized nation by the year 2030

Volatility Marked by upward and downward swings as a result of forces at play

Western Powers Nations with a largely Anglo-Saxon heritage

1 Introduction

I suspect that if you were to carry out a quick survey by asking the residents of Nairobi what the Nairobi Securities Exchange is, you would get various responses, many of which would leave you baffled. You would hear answers like it is a large company in Nairobi, a large security firm in the city, an exchange program for students and many such grandiose ideas. The point is, most people in Kenya – as in nations around Africa – have never heard of their nation's stock market and have no idea what it means and does. At a time this continent is poised for economic takeoff, this is regrettable and must be addressed at once.

The continent of Africa has faced upheavals in every sphere of life. We have experienced economic meltdowns and stagnated growth because of poor political leadership, inability to compete global conglomerates, a business environment skewed in favor of developed nations and not third world economies and many other factors of our own making. In the social sphere, our motherland has had to cope with the growing westernization of approaches in culture, religion – which has caused remarkable transformation in Africa by injecting permissiveness, rugged individualism and a philosophical tilt in the direction of humanism.

But it is, perhaps, in the sphere of politics that the nations of Africa have faced the most critical challenges. Having been colonized by Western powers for so long – and only gaining independence in the sixties – these nations replaced colonial brutality with black rule that was characterized by ineptness, murder, civil wars and rolling instability. In Uganda, the military coup that brought Idi Amin Dada to power also ushered in repression and assassinations on a scale Africa had never seen before. In Zaire, Mobutu Sese Seko presided over a brutal dictatorship that plundered the wealth of that nation and left it in utter ruin. And in Somalia, Siad Barre's autocratic rule resulted in the nation's degeneration into a civil war that has never ended.

As if that were not enough, the sudden emergence of global terror as a factor in modern life has complicated life in Africa – just as it has complicated it globally. In the Eastern Africa region, the terror outfit known as Al Shabaab has staged repeated attacks in Kenya and

Uganda, causing investor anxiety and general fear in the nations around the Horn of Africa. In the Western African region, Boko Haram has staged daring attacks in Nigeria and has become a menace to the regional economic bloc ECOWAS. The net impact of these terror attacks is that investor confidence is undermined locally and in global business circles.

At a time Africa is set to play an increasingly major role in the global economy, it is critical to study and understand the role a stock exchange plays in shaping thought in business circles and influencing investor confidence. And this is important because there was a time most people in Africa, especially in Kenya, thought of investors as foreigners who flew into Nairobi with loads of cash and met the President at State House, then established a posh office in the trendiest area of the city. Unfortunately, that perception has been slow to die – many of us still don't see locals as serious investors.

The reason this must trouble each of us is because lack of investment – local and foreign – will continue to deny us the growth we need to lift our nations into the prestigious club of developed nations. The projected timeframes for Kenya to become an industrialized nation, dubbed Vision 2030, can only be achieved if a vibrant middle class is created by harnessing all factors that influence economic growth to play their positive role in birthing that very kind of a society. In an increasingly optimistic and predictable Africa, this is an outcome that is not only possible, but must be strived toward.

This book is designed to demystify the stock market and help the citizens of our various nations understand how its buoyance or lack thereof affects life. We all have to come away with the knowledge that stock markets the world over – individually and collectively – play a critical role in national economies and on the global level. This is because they provide:

- Long-term capital for investment,
- An avenue for those with excess cash or savings to invest,
- A market for holders of equity to trade, hence providing liquidity of investments.

The performance of a given stock market is influenced by two critical factors:

a. Activities of a government and
b. General performance of the economy.

These two factors are important for our understanding of the role stock markets play. We will examine them and explain their interaction with other factors that influence economic growth. Various studies have been carried out in the United States and in Britain to examine the performance of their respective stock markets before and after elections. Similar studies have been done to focus on a stock market's performance based on the party of the President or Prime Minister in power.

Of course in the United States and in Great Britain this is possible because political parties have set policies and are expected to act in accordance with those policies. Investors are guided by predictability because they know what to expect from the Laborites, Tories and the Conservatives – in Great Britain. In the United States, the Republicans and Democrats run on platforms that have guided party policy and interactions over the years.

Predictability, however, is not something many African nations have enjoyed. Political parties on the continent are weak and serve more as vehicles to power than tools for the betterment of life after elections. They are tribal, shallow in ideological depth and are run like private firms – with the head of the party being the man or woman to watch. This is the reason Africa has been held back by the Big Man syndrome and personality cults around the Head of State.

The studies I have alluded to indicate that the stock market reacts differently based on the party of the President elected in the United States, but that there is no reaction in Great Britain. It says something remarkable about Great Britain's maturity as an economy that politics has minimal impact in shaping market direction. The United States is just as mature and indeed, there is an argument to be made about the need to maintain a healthy interaction between politics and markets.

The Nairobi Securities Exchange is one of the oldest and among the most established stock markets in Africa. There are many parameters that would determine size:

- Turnover,
- Number of companies listed, and
- Market capitalization of all companies listed.

The above points may cause ranking to differ. For the purposes of this discussion, however, the Nairobi Securities Exchange is the one we will use as a reference point. At the completion of my study in 2008, four general elections had taken place in Kenya under the multiparty system – all of which had affected the NSE in one way or another. In the study I carried out, I analyzed the performance of the stock exchange before and after the general elections of 1992, 1997, 2002 and 2007. To arrive at patterns and projections, I used:

- Line graphs,
- Percentages,
- Mean,
- Variance and other statistical measures.

In the end, what I realized was that Kenyans – and the people of Africa – have to understand the great impact a stock market has on the quality of their life. They need to realize that the stock market is a clear indicator of how the nation is being led and how investors regard the direction in which the nation is going. It also says something about the place a given nation occupies at the global table of brotherhood. In this regard, President Barack Obama's historic visit to Kenya must be seen within the context of growing confidence in the economy, politics and projected future of our nation.

The approach in this book is not a heavy-lifting academic one – that will defeat our purpose. The idea is to give Kenyans, and our African brothers and sisters, a new tool to use in assessing the performance of the government and their own quality of life. A responsible government will create an environment that opens up space for brisk business and investment; an irresponsible or clueless one will preside over the decay of institutions and usher in repression because it lacks imagination.

The future looks great for Kenya and for Africa, but it can only be so if we all do our part in democratizing this continent and holding our leaders to account for each action. We have to strive for a society that runs on the basis of the four core pillars of:

a. A vibrant press.
b. An independent Judiciary.
c. A functioning Legislature and
d. A responsible Executive.

The Military – having played a key role in the narrative of Africa – cannot be regarded in isolation, but the time has come when our men in uniform must never be allowed to seize power by the barrel of a gun. The activities of Africa's military rulers like General Sani Abacha, Field Marshall Idi Amin Dada and others have been deeply irresponsible, painful and stagnating. Similarly, the activities of rebel leaders like Sudan's Dr. Riek Machar, Angola's Jonas Savimbi and Uganda's Kony have served no useful purpose other than to destabilize economic growth and cause unending misery to people.

Discussions in this book are bold, vibrant and healthy. They are designed only to open the eyes of the African people to the need for greater accountability by holding leaders to the promises they make on the campaign trail.

If indeed African democracy has come of age, its impact must now be felt in the quality of life the people of Africa live. In Kenya, it begins by analyzing trends at the Nairobi Securities exchange. So what is the NSE?

Questions

The questions below are designed to recap key elements in this chapter. An in-depth study of issues raised in the chapter is recommended.

1. The performance of a given stock market is influenced by two critical factors.

    a. Name these two factors
    b. Discuss how these factors affect performance of the stock market

2. Discuss the impact of predictability on performance of the stock market.
3. Name the four core pillars of democracy.

2 Nairobi Securities Exchange

Defining the Nairobi Securities Exchange

The Nairobi Securities Exchange, also known as the NSE, is an institution that deals in the exchange of securities issued by publicly-quoted companies, or firms, and the government. A stock market like the NSE is part of a broader market referred to as the financial market. A financial market is a market where financial assets or financial instruments are traded and the instruments entitle a holder to a claim to future cash. In this regard, the entity that agrees to make future cash payment is called the issuer of financial assets while the owner of the financial asset is referred to as the investor (Fabozzi, 1995).

The terminologies used to describe the stock market could be confusing, but what they mean is this – that a person with money to invest will identify a publicly traded company to invest his or her money in anticipation that at a future date, that company will have made profits from which payment in cash would be given to him or her. That payment will be proportionate to the size of investment originally made.

It is critical to understand that the claim a holder of a financial asset is entitled to may be either a fixed shilling amount, may vary or may be residual. Reilly (1997) carried out research in this area of financial market and made an effort to describe his findings. He says that in the case of a fixed or varying shilling amount, the financial asset it referred to as a debt instrument.

An equity claim, which is also known as residual claim, obligates the issuer of the financial asset to pay the holder an amount based on earnings – if any – after holders of debt instruments have been paid. An example of an equity claim in common stock. Debt and preferred stock that pay a fixed income are called fixed income instruments (Reilly, 1997).

Obviously the research done by Reilly was based on the dynamics of a dollar market – in the United States. That financial market is highly developed and deals with a lot more variables than the Nairobi one, but key elements apply to such markets the world over. What Reilly and

Fabozzi discovered about Western markets apply to markets around the world – including the developing ones across Africa.

Historical Background

Most readers of this book will be stunned to learn that in Kenya, dealing in shares started in the 1920s, when the country was still a British colony. In those days, there were no formal markets, no rules and no regulations to govern stock broking activities. Trading took place on a gentleman's agreement in which standard commissions were charged with clients being obligated to honor their contractual commitments of making good delivery and settling relevant costs.

Muga, studying this historical background in 1974, says that in 1951 a respected estate agent by the name Francis Drummond – he was British – established the first professional stockbroking firm. He later approached the then Finance Minister in Kenya, Sir Ernest Vasey, and impressed upon him the need to set up a stock exchange in East Africa. The two officials took it upon themselves to discuss this matter with the London Stock Exchange officials in July 1953. Officials in the LSE saw no reason to decline the request and thus the Nairobi Stock Exchange was set up as an overseas stock exchange (Muga, 1974).

The fifties were the difficult days in Kenya, when British authorities locked up Africans in the highlands into reserves so that land was left for them to farm. This act of disinheriting Africans of their ancestral land led to the popular revolt known as the Mau Mau uprising. It says something about the British settlers' confidence in ruling Kenya for years that they could set up a stock market right in the middle of such a threatening revolt. Of course they had superior firepower, which could have made them feel secure about their future in Kenya.

On their website www.nse.co.ke, the Nairobi Securities Exchange records that the body was constituted as a voluntary association of stockbrokers, registered under the Societies Act in 1954. This was at the height of the insurgency, a time the Agikuyu of Central Kenya were up in arms about their land. Led by men like Dedan Kimathi, Waruhiu Itote and others, they attacked the settlers and hid in the bushes. The idea was to make the area so insecure that most settlers would of their own volition leave – if they didn't, they would get killed.

In 1991, the Nairobi Stock Exchange was incorporated under the Companies Act of Kenya as a company limited by guarantee and without a share capital. Today the NSE is among the largest securities exchange in Africa. NSE was recently listed as a public company.

Performance of a Stock Market

As noted earlier, stock markets perform a wide range of economic and political functions while offering trading, investment, speculation, hedging, and even arbitrage opportunities. They serve as a mechanism for price discovery and information dissemination, but also provide vehicles for raising finances for companies – and are frequently pivotal elements in the success of financial centers. They are used to implement privatization programs and often play an important role in the development of emerging economies (Lee, 1998).

The performance of a stock market is influenced by a number of factors, which are directly tied to the way a nation is governed. Indeed, we already noted that the activities of governments and the general performance of the economy are key factors. It is also important to take into account other contributing factors to a stock market's rise. Monetary and fiscal measures enacted by various agencies of the national government influences the aggregate economy of a nation (Mendelson, 1976).

In the early days of a post-independence Africa, many nations, which had just gotten rid of colonial officials, found themselves unprepared for the task of managing the various sectors of the nations they had just liberated.

Lack of needed skills in enacting sound monetary and fiscal policies led to a predictable faltering in growth and setback in performance of stock markets in these nations. Mandelson (1976) observes that the resulting economic conditions from bad governance and flawed fiscal and monetary policies will inevitably influence all industries and companies within the economies negatively. Such negative influencing will in turn affect the stock market negatively (Mendelson, 1976).

Other key factors that affect stock market performance include:

- Availability of other investment assets,
- Change in composition of investors, and
- Market sentiments.

All the factors we have noted as key to stock market performance are directly tied to how well a nation is governed. In Africa, where the post-independence landscape was riddle with civil wars, military coups, ineptness of the dictators and natural calamities, stock markets responded to these uncertainties by shrinking, stagnating or not being birthed at all. Nations like Chad, Somalia and Uganda got caught up in civil wars that made it difficult for a stock market to emerge and thrive.

As is to be expected, market sentiment is a key factor in the performance of a stock market. In discussing sentiment, we need to look at the major issues that play into fostering a positive, reassuring sentiment:

a. **Political stability**. We've already identified Chad, Somalia and Uganda as nations where political instability created negative sentiment. Investors are always reluctant to invest their monies in a nation or economy where the prospect of colossal losses looms large. Markets thrive in stable, predictable environments; not in environments where unpredictability restricts trade and makes future forecasts as gloomy as a cloudy night. A stable government is one that entertains:
   - An independent Judiciary,
   - A free Press,
   - A robust Legislature,
   - A vibrant civil society
   - A strong private sector, being the engine of economic growth,
   - A responsive Executive, and
   - A Military with a civilian (Head of State) at its command apex.

b. **Monetary and fiscal policies**. Most nations that will foster stable environment for a thriving stock market will inevitably augment political stability with sound monetary and fiscal policies. There is need to create a sense that a nation's assets and finances are managed in a prudent manner by men and women who are professionals in the area of economic management. In the years after African nations got independent, many leaders brought in relatives and friends to sit in offices they were ill-equipped to run. It was no wonder that policies related to the economy were set in a haphazard manner and most nations crawled to a halt – then turned to the World Bank and the International Monetary Fund to seek help. The net impact of this was to release Africa into the open arms of world systems eager to usher in a period of neocolonialism. By borrowing heftily from the twin Bretton Woods institutions, are we still stuck in that realm of neocolonialism or have we evolved into our own masters? Can we finally chart our own destiny as Africans without reliance on foreign powers and institutions to provide funds, expertise and oversight?

c. **Capacity-building**. Capacity-building has become a watchword for continued training and equipping of professionals and other workers in each sector of an economy. Once again, capacity-building has to go hand-in-hand with responsive governance, and sound monetary and fiscal policies. For an economy to grow and show the promise of future expansion, workers at all levels must be trained to acquire new skills that reflect anticipated growth in the economy.

Various authors have examined the immediate market reaction to a presidential election. Most of these studies were conducted in the United States, but may provide clues to global trends regarding elections. In the United States, these studies show that the immediate market reaction to a Republican presidential win is always positive while a Democratic win is always negative – which means decrease in stock index (Siegel, 1998 and Riley, 1980).

In spite of this, the party effect, in which popular wisdom assert that the stock market prefers Republican presidents to Democratic ones turns out to be false in the long run. Evidence supports the opposite proposition – that stocks eventually perform better under a Democratic rather than a Republican president (Jones, 2002).

In Kenya, the elections – which gave rise to the very first independent Kenyan government – were held in the month of May 1963, under the supervision of the the colonial government. The 1969, 1974, 1979, 1983 and 1988 were held under a one-party system. Those five elections produced a closed system, where predictability was possible in terms of peace and political orderliness, but not in market projection. The one-party dictatorship that emerged created an unstable environment where the government was firmly and ruthlessly in control, thus seeing no need to be either responsive or answerable to the electorate. Institutions got run down, worker morale plummeted and the economy stagnated because of poor governance. The nation eventually ground to a halt.

The 1992, 1997, 2002, 2007 and 2013 elections were held under a multiparty system after the Constitution was changed to reintroduce multiparty politics in Kenya (Commonwealth, 2006). Promulgation of the Kenyan Constitution in 2010 further liberalized politics in Kenya, creating institutions and systems vibrant enough to act as solid checks and balances to possible abuses by one or the other arms of government.

To get a sense of trends in the years between and during elections, we need to work with graphs that track performance of the stock market.

Here they are:

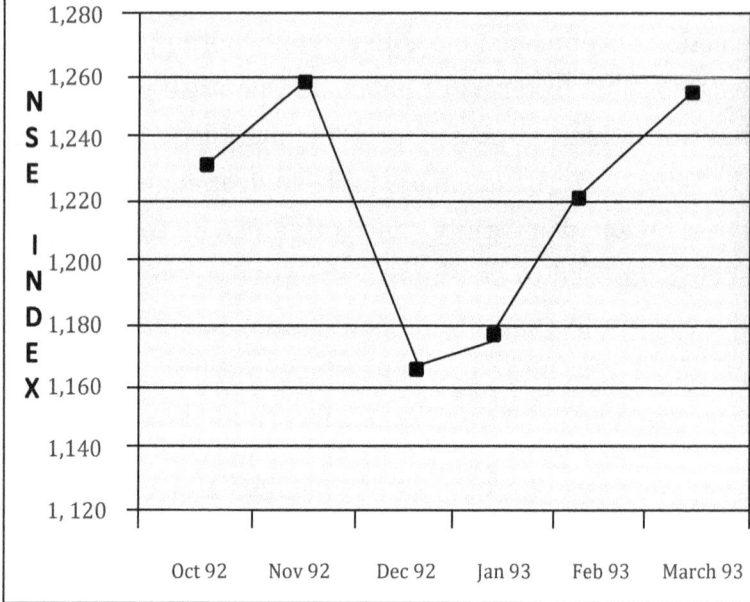

NSE Index – 1992 Election

Chart 1.1: Market Performance for three month period before and after elections

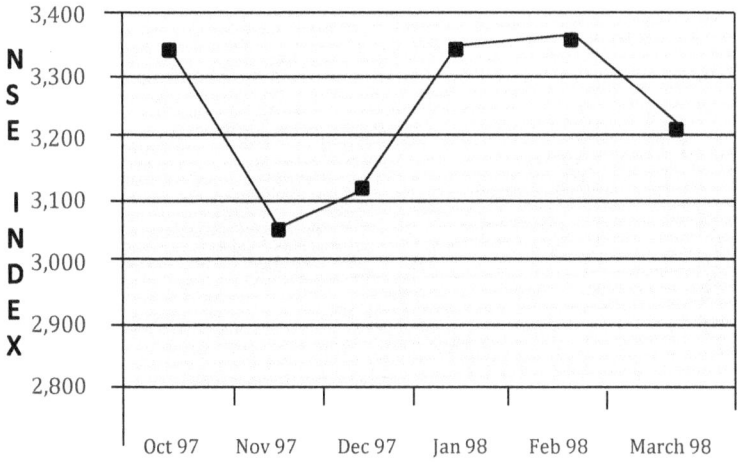

NSE Index – 1997 Election

Chart 1.2: Market Performance for three month period before and after elections

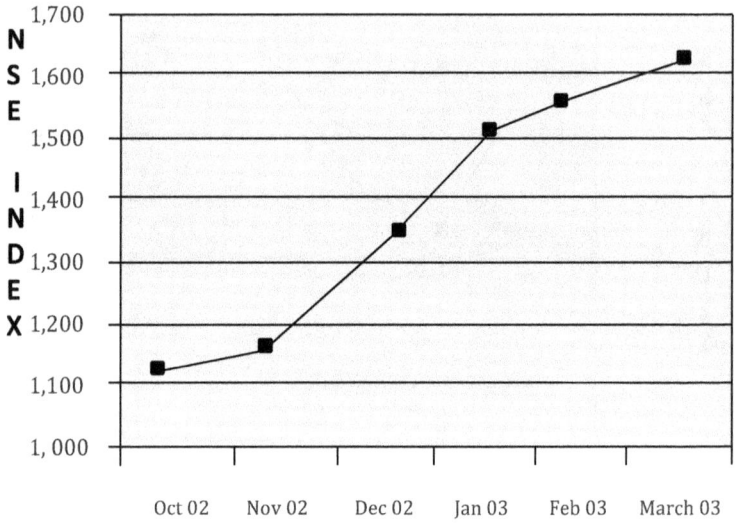

NSE Index – 2002 Election

Chart 1.3: Market Performance for three month period before and after elections

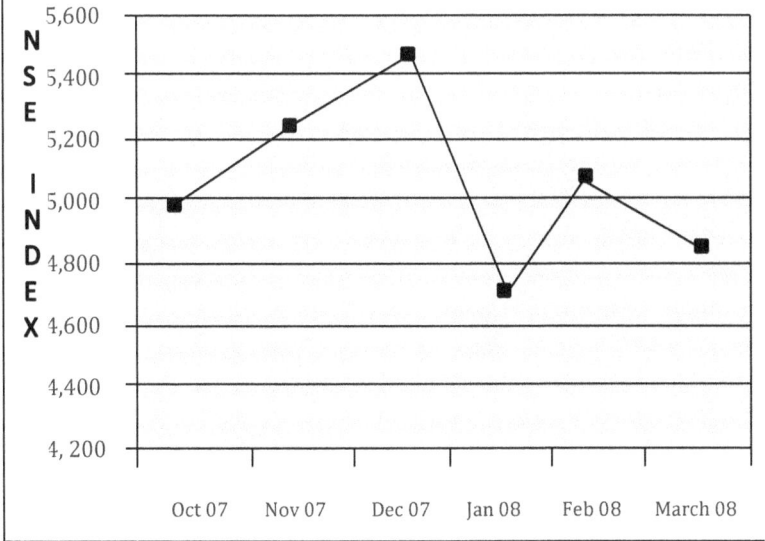

NSE Index – 2007 Election

Chart 1.4: Market Performance for three month period before
and after elections

The question one would ask, therefore, is this: has the emergence of a number of parties as contenders for power given Kenya a platform to usher in ideology-based governance that could affect market performance one way or the other? More importantly, who are the conservatives and who are the liberals in Kenya? How do their policies affect the common man?

In the next chapter, we are going to discuss indicators prevalently deployed in stock markets to determine performance. We will also consider the structural changes that have been implemented in the recent past to bring the NSE into compliance with the best market practices.

Questions

The questions below are designed to recap key elements in this chapter. An in-depth study of issues raised in the chapter is recommended.

1. Define the Nairobi Securities Exchange.
2. Who is:
   a. An issuer of financial assets?
   b. An investor?
3. What is the significance of Francis Drummond in the history of Kenya's stock market?
4. What was the effect of a one-party system on the growth of Kenya's stock market?
5. How have stock markets in Africa fared under authoritarian and dictatorial presidencies?

References

Commonwealth. (2006). *The Report of the 2002 Kenya General Election Common Wealth Observer Group*.

Fabozzi F. & Modigiliani F. (1995). *Capital Market Institutions and Instruments.* New Jersey: Prentice Hall, Inc.

Jones, T. (2002). Presidential Election Cycles and Stock Market Returns*. Conference Paper for the American Academy and Finance.* New York: McGraw Hill.

Lee R. (1998). *What is an Exchange? The Automation, Management and Regulation of Financial Markets.* New York: Oxford University Press Inc.

Mendelson M. & Robbins S. (1976*). Investment Analysis and Security Markets.* New York: Basic Books, Inc.

Muga D.N. (1994). *The Nairobi Stock Exchange; its History, Organization and Role in the Kenyan Economy. Unpublished* MBA Dissertation, University of Nairobi.

Reilly F. & Brown C. (1997). Investment Analysis and Portfolio Management 5th Edition. New Jersey: Prentice Hall, Inc.

Siegel, J. J. (1998). *Stocks for the Long Run*. New York: McGraw Hill.

http://www.nse.co.ke Nairobi Stock Exchange Website

The NSE Prophecy

3 Stock Market Performance Indicators

A stock market is like a baby. When a baby is born, the early days of life are critical because of fragility of the toddler and the dangers existent around it. For doctors to be sure a toddler is developing well, certain milestones have to be reached and crossed safely. This is the case with a stock market as well. In the beginning, the Nairobi Securities Exchange was brought into existence as a toddler, but over the years it has grown to take its place as one of the most established stock markets in Africa. In spite of such extraordinary growth, like a child, the NSE has to be observed periodically and a number of critical measures applied to determine how well growth is taking place.

In this chapter, we want to look at the many indicators one needs to watch in determining whether the stock market is growing or stagnating.

Performance Indicators

The prices of stocks around the world do not move together in an exact manner. This is because economic systems in which stock markets are located have dissimilar environments in terms of:

- Taxation,
- Industrial growth,
- Political stability, and
- Monetary policies.

Stock markets may experience a general increase in price level, referred to as a *bull* market, or general decrease in price level, referred to as a *bear* market. They may also experience stagnant prices or the seismic wave of sudden big price movements downward – which is known as a market crash. In the life of a child, this would be the equivalent of a debilitating ailment.

There are many stock market indexes that chart and measure the performance of the various stock markets. In every country where stock trading takes place, there is usually at least one index that measures general price movements. If a given country has more than one stock exchange, each exchange normally has its own index. It is also the case that new organizations and financial advisory services create new indexes (Fabozzi, 1995).

Simiyu is a Kenyan researcher familiar with the ebbs and flows of a stock market. Carrying out his study of stocks in 1992, he discovered that a stock market index is one of the most widely used measures of stock performance. Investors hold portfolios of many assets, but it is cumbersome to follow progress on each security in the portfolio. It is prudent, therefore, to observe the entire market under the notion that their portfolio moved the same direction as the aggregate market. The market index such as the NSE index is used to observe total returns for an aggregate market and those computed returns are to judge performance of individual portfolios. The assumption is that randomly selecting a large number of stocks from the total market, the investor should be able to experience a rate of return comparable to the market (Simiyu, 1992).

Market capitalization is another measure of stock market performance. It is used to measure market movements. It measures the total value of stocks in a particular stock market by aggregating the market value of stocks. The market stock price of each share is multiplied by outstanding shares and market values of all stocks added to obtain the market capitalization.

Otuke, in 2006, analyzed the behavior of markets and observed that changes in market capitalization occur due to fluctuations in share prices or issuance of new shares or bonus and this implies more activity at the stock market that may signal more investment taking place. Market turnover is another measure different from market capitalization. It shows cash inflows and outflows in the stock market. It is based on the actively traded shares and a change occurs due to fluctuation in share prices or number of shares traded in a day (Otuke, 2006).

These indicators, though, are dependent on factors that determine how a stock market performs. In this next segment, I want us to look at these factors under a subtitle that substitutes the word factors with the word determinates.

Determinants of performance of stock markets

The performance of stock markets is influenced by a number of factors – key among them being the activities of governments and the general performance of the economy. Monetary and fiscal measures enacted by various agencies of national governments influence the aggregate economies of those countries. The resulting economic conditions influence all industries and companies within the economies positively or negatively.

These, in turn, affect the performance of stock markets (Reilly, 1997).

Fiscal policy incentives such as tax cuts can encourage spending, whereas additional taxes on income, petroleum products, cigarettes, and alcoholic beverages discourage spending. Increase or decrease in government spending on defense, training programs or on infrastructure also influences the general economy. All policies of this nature influence the business environment directly for firms that rely directly on those expenditures. In addition, government spending has a strong multiplier effect. For example, increases in road construction increases the demand for earthmoving equipment and also for road construction materials. As a result of this, in addition to construction workers, employees in the industries that supply equipment and materials have more to spend on consumer goods. This ripple effect raises demand for consumer goods, which affects another set of suppliers and the ripple rolls on.

Monetary policy produces similar economic changes. A restrictive monetary policy that reduces the growth rate of money supply reduces the supply of funds for working capital and for expansion of business. Alternatively, a restrictive monetary policy that targets interest rates would raise the market interest rates and thus the firm's cost of capital and make it more expensive for individuals to finance home mortgage and purchase of other durable goods such as motor vehicles and electronic appliances. Monetary policy, therefore, affects all segments of the economy including stock markets and an economy's relationship with other economies (Mendelson, 1976).

Inflation is another factor that affects the performance of stock markets. Inflation causes differences between real and nominal interest rates and changes the spending and saving behavior of consumers and firms. Unexpected changes in the rate of inflation make it difficult for firms to plan and this inhibits growth and innovation. Beyond the impact of a domestic economy, differential inflation and interest rates influence the trade balance between countries and exchange rate for currencies (Reilly, 1997).

In addition to monetary and fiscal policy actions, there are events that may produce changes in the business environment that may add to the uncertainty of sales and earnings expectations and therefore the risk premium required by investors. These events, as envisaged by Mendelson (1976), include:

- War,
- Political upheavals within or outside a nation, and
- International monetary devaluation.

Mendelson (1976) goes on to say stock prices are based on the potential earning power of corporations, a factor that is influenced directly by economic conditions. As a result, fluctuations in the general level of stock market performance reflect investor consensus concerning the economic outlook. Over a period of years, it is logical to expect a close relationship between business activity and changes in stock prices.

Availability of other investment alternatives to shares traded on the stock market affect the stock market's performance. Stock markets compete for investment capital with other asset classes on the national stage. On the NSE, these include:

- Corporate bonds,
- Government bonds,
- Treasury bills,
- Real estate, and
- Foreign equity among others.

The relation between demand for government bonds and treasury bills has been inversely proportional to equities and this relationship plays a very important role in the capital market. For example, interest rates between 2004 and 2006 were relatively down, resulting in the Bull Run.

that was experienced at the Nairobi Stock Exchange in those two years (www.nse.co.ke).

Changes in investor composition also affect stock market performance. A supply and demand for security change over time, different types of investors are attracted to the market. If the risk preferences of these new investors are not as those of current investors, the required rate of return tends to shift. Accordingly, price relationship will change independently of any modification in earnings expectations. For example, the demographics of investors that have shaped the Nairobi Stock Exchange relates to two dynamics:

a. Increased middle-aged investors who are peak earners, and
b. An increase in older investors tending to pull out of the market in order to meet the demands of retirement.

The hypothesis here is that the greater the proportion of middle-aged investors among the investing population in our capital market, the greater the demand for equities and the higher the valuation multiples like price earnings ratio (Reilly, 1997).

Market sentiment, also referred to as the psychology of market participants, affects stock market performance.

The NSE Prophecy

Market sentiment is often subjective, biased and reliably obstinate. The uncertain mass reaction of individuals to developments affecting the stock market is one of the factors that handicap stock market forecasting. A mild market flurry caused by a spurt in business activity may generate a wave of buying enthusiasm that raises stock to boom levels. As an indication of this tendency, from January 1967 through December 1968 the American Stock Exchange Index more than doubled in the face of a business advance of about ten percent. The starry-eyed optimism of buyers who believe that prices are heading indefinitely higher may produce substantial advances that are not reasonably justified by underlying financial considerations. On the other hand, pervasive investor gloom, generated by economic or political uncertainties, could drive prices to levels that appear equally unjustified by standard financial tests (Mendelson, 1976).

The occasionally irrational attitude of buyers was noted by John Maynard Keynes, who said that professional investors "are concerned, not with what an investment is really worth to a man who buys it for keeps, but with what the market will value it at, under the influence of mass psychology, three months or a year hence." This explains the relatively positive performance of the NSE, which is domiciled in a nation that has experienced long periods of peace and predictability.

That said, psychological factors that motivate individuals to buy and sell stocks are difficult to evaluate and make hazardous the role of stock market forecasters. They, however, present opportunities for substantial profits and cannot be ignored by the more adventuresome investor (Mandelson, 1976). This irrational attitude of buyers, due to politically-motivated activities before or after an election, is a factor to watch before, during and after an election because it is bound to affect stock market performance. In Kenya, the election of 2002 was a time of great jubilation and stocks rallied. There was a general feeling that Kenya had united. In 2007/08, the nation fractured along ethnic lines and the market responded with gloom.

It was, perhaps, in preparation for a stable and modern market that the government envisioned a need to make structural changes in the Nairobi Securities Exchange. It is with those changes I want us to close this chapter.

Kenya Stock Market Structural Changes

In 1980, the Kenyan government realized the need to design and implement policy reforms to foster sustainable economic development with an efficient and stable financial system. In particular, it set out to:

- Enhance the role of the private sector in the economy,
- Reduce the demands of public enterprises on the exchequer,
- Rationalize the operations of the public enterprises sector to broaden the base of ownership and enhance capital market development.

The International Finance Corporation and the Central Bank of Kenya carried out a study on "Development of Money and Capital Markets in Kenya." That 1984 study became a blueprint for structural reforms in the financial markets, which culminated in the formation of a regulatory body – The Capital Markets Authority (CMA), in 1989, to assist in the creation of a conducive environment for the growth and development of the country's capital markets (IFC/CBK, 1984). In 1988, Kenya Commercial Bank (KBC) became the first company to privatize through the Nairobi Stock Exchange. This was after the government successfully sold 20% of its holding in the bank.

In 1991, the NSE was registered under the Companies Act and phased out the "Call Over" trading system in favor of the floor-based Outcry System. The NSE 20-share Index recorded an all-round high of 5030 points on February 18, 1994. The NSE was rated by the International Finance Corporation as the best-performing market in the world with a return of 179% in dollar terms. Extensive modernization exercise was undertaken, including a move to more spacious premises at the Nation Center in July 1994, setting up a computerized delivery and settlement system (DASS) and a modern information center. For the first time in its history, the number of stockbrokers increased with the licensing of eight new brokers (www.nse.co.ke).

The Kenyan government relaxed restrictions on foreign ownership in locally-controlled companies, subject to an aggregate limit of 20% and an individual 2.5% in 1995. These were later doubled to 40% and 5% respectively in the June 1995 budget to help encourage foreign portfolio investments. The entire Exchange Control Act was repealed in December 1995. Seven more stockbrokers were licensed, bringing the number to twenty from the original six – one of which has survived since its inception in 1954. Commission rates were reduced considerably from 2.5% to between 2% and 1% on a sliding scale and 0.05% for all fixed interest securities.

In 1996, the largest share issue in the then history of NSE, the privatization of Kenya Airways, came to the market and more than 110,000 shareholders acquired a stake in the airline. The Kenya airways Privatization team was awarded the World Bank Award for excellence for 1996 for being a model success story in the divestiture of state-owned enterprises.

In 1998, the government expanded the scope for foreign investment by introducing incentives for capital markets growth, including the setting up of tax-free Venture Capital Funds, removal of Capital Gains Tax on insurance companies' investments, allowance of beneficial ownership by foreigners in local stockbrokers and fund managers and the envisaged licensing of Dealing Firms to improve market liquidity.

It is important to note that in addition to the existing NSE indices, expansion of the stock market made it inevitable to have additional indices. We, thus, now have NSE 20 Share Index and NSE All Share Index (NASI).

This has been a heavy discussion, but a necessary one. It puts us in the frame of mind to finally discuss the impact of elections on the performance of a stock market.

We will look at foreign as well as our own market to assess the similarities and differences – and decide whether there is any significant lesson we may learn from the more developed markets abroad.

Questions

The questions below are designed to recap key elements in this chapter. An in-depth study of issues raised in the chapter is recommended.

1. Name the four key indicators of a market performance.
2. What is:
   a. A bull market?
   b. A bear market?
   c. Market crash?
3. Define:
   a. Fiscal discipline
   b. Monetary policy
   c. Taxation
   d. Inflation
   e. Risk premium.
4. Discuss the structural changes that have taken place in the Kenyan stock market since the 1980s.

References

Fabozzi F. & Modigiliani F. (1995). *Capital Market Institutions and Instruments.* New Jersey: Prentice Hall, Inc.

Mendelson M. & Robbins S. (1976*). Investment Analysis and Security Markets.* New York: Basic Books, Inc.

Otuke, J. (2006). Impact of Central Depository System on the Performance of NSE –*Unpublished MBA Dissertation, University of Nairobi.*

Reilly F. & Brown C. (1997). Investment Analysis and Portfolio
Management 5th Edition. New Jersey: Prentice Hall, Inc.

Simiyu, M. (1992). Measuring Market Performance of the NSE –
Unpublished MBA dissertation, University of Nairobi.

http://www.nse.co.ke Nairobi Stock Exchange Website

4 The Role of Stock Markets

frican nations have developed at a much slower pace than their Western counterparts, but it is not until one has a deep understanding of stock markets that one is able to assess the incredible distance nations across this continent have to cover to catch up with the ones labeled developed nations. Stock markets are jittery organisms that respond to the slightest indication of trouble and are only happy when peace and predictability abound. Underdevelopment of African stock markets is, therefore, indicative of absence of cohesiveness, underdevelopment in infrastructure and poor governance.

In this chapter, we are going to discuss the role of stock markets in detail so that we may establish how the success or failure of one is determined by the winds of strife that blow in a nation. The operational question is: what is the role of a stock market? But instead of a point by point discussion, we want to adopt a narrative style, one that draws in key elements as it opens up thoughts about the role of a stock market.

Role of a stock market

The major role stock markets have played – and continue to play in many economies – is to promote a culture of thrift or saving. The fact that institutions exist where savers can safely invest their money and also earn a return is an incentive for people to consume less and save more. In Kenya, the stock market has contributed to increase in the level of saving – the relevant question may be: who is doing the saving? What class of people?

The growth of related financial services sector such as unit trusts, investment clubs, insurance, pension, and provident fund schemes nurtures the spirit of saving and must be encouraged. Once monies are saved in one of the service sectors mentioned, the stock market steps in to transfer those savings to investment in productive enterprises as an alternative to keeping the savings idle. The idea is to use the savings to make more money rather than have them sit still in a savings box.

It should be appreciated that in as much as an economy can have savings, lack of established mechanisms for channeling those savings into profitable activities that create wealth would lead to misallocation or waste of those savings (www.nse.co.ke). The upshot of this matter is clear – that saving without investing is a fool's errand and won't stimulate the economy to grow. Encouraging a culture of saving for the mere sake of saving in a less developed financial market may indeed lead to economic stagnation and needs to be discouraged. An economy is bound to suffer slow growth and may eventually get crippled if a stock market is not fed the savings accrued so that wealth is created within a nation.

A robust stock market assists in the rational and efficient allocation of capital – which is a scarce resource. The fact that capital is scarce means systems have to be developed so that capital is allocated to the most deserving user. An efficient stock market sector will have the expertise, the institutions and means to prioritize access to capital by competing users so that an economy manages to realize maximum output at the least cost. This is what global economists refer to as the optimum production level. If an economy does not have efficient financial markets, there is always the risk that the scarce capital could be channeled to nonproductive investments as opposed to productive ones, leading to wastage of resources and precipitating economic decline (Lee, 1998).

The existence of a stock market always promotes higher standards of accounting, resource management and transparency in the management of business. This is because financial markets encourage the separation of owners of capital, on the one hand, from managers of capital, on the other. This separation is an important one because people who have money may not necessarily have the best business ideas, and the people with the best business ideas may not necessarily have money. Because the two sides need each other, a stock exchange becomes the all-important link (www.nse.co.ke).

It is regrettable that not too many Kenyans know what the stock market is – and many more have no idea what it can do for them. A private company in need of capital for expansion, for example, can approach the Capital Market Authority (CMA) and the Nairobi Stock Exchange (NSE) to raise funds through an Initial Public Offer (IPO). This arrangement is a symbiotic one because it benefits both parties in this manner: the manager of capital, who is the entrepreneur, is able to access capital to turn his idea into a reality, while the owners of capital, who are the shareholders, receive a return on their investment without having to report to work at the company – or as the Americans would say, without breaking a sweat. It works for all involved, but more importantly, it works for the nation by expanding the economy (www.nse.co.ke).

Improving access to finance for different types of users by providing flexibility for customization is an important role of the stock market. This is made possible as the financial sector allows the different users of capital to raise capital in ways that are suited to meeting their specific needs. For example, established companies can raise short-term finance through commercial paper; small companies can raise long-term capital by selling shares; the government and even municipal councils can raise funds by floating various types of bonds as an alternative to foreign borrowing (www.nse.co.ke).

Investors are provided with an efficient mechanism to liquidate their investments in securities through a stock market. The very fact that investors are certain of the possibility of selling out what they hold – as and when they wish to – is a major incentive for investment as it guarantees mobility of capital in the purchase of assets. The interactions of buyers and sellers in a stock market determine the price of trade assets; or, equivalently, the required return on a financial asset. The inducement for firms to acquire funds depends on the required return that investor demand, and it is this future of stock market that signals how funds in the economy should be allocated among financial assets. This is called the price discovery process, as Fabozzi noted (Fabozzi, 1995).

Fabozzi (1995) goes on to say that reduction of the search and information costs of transacting at the stock market is key to facilitating growth of the market. Search costs represent explicit costs, such as money spent to advertise the desire to sell or purchase a financial asset, and implicit costs, such as the value of time spent in locating counterparty. The presence of some form of organized stock market reduces search costs. Information costs are those entailed with assessing the investment merits of a financial asset; that is, the amount and the likelihood of the cash flow reasonably expected to be generated.

A stock market facilitates equity financing as opposed to debt financing. Companies can raise equity through initial public offers, secondary offers or rights issues. Debt financing has been the undoing of many enterprises in the developed and developing countries – especially in recessionary periods. At times, a company in need of funds for expansion may not be able to use debt-financing if it has a high debt to equity ratio. That's why equity financing provides a better solution in such cases (www.nse.co.ke).

The last point to make on the role of a stock market is this: avenues for public floatation of private companies and government-owned entities, which in turn allow greater growth and increase of the supply of assets available for long-term investment, are available at the stock market. This leads to wealth redistribution from state and private companies to the investing public since they can share in the returns of the privatized entities. The establishment of an efficient stock market is, thus, indispensable for any economy that is keen on using scarce capital resources to achieve economic growth (www.nse.co.ke).

A stock market, as we have established, is central to a nation's economic growth and is an indicator of a nation's health. Kenya has benefited immensely from the relative peace and stability experienced over the years. The silent policy of *stability at all cost* – adopted by the nation's presidents, and supported by Western powers with a stake in Kenya's stability – has paid off. The fear of total breakdown into anarchy has goaded world powers and Kenya's leaders to adopt a form of democracy that is incremental in the nature of freedoms it accords the people. It may be faulted, but it has worked.

It is this stability that has enabled the NSE to emerge among the most established stock markets in Africa. As Kenya continues to strengthen pivotal institutions geared toward sound management of public resources and excellence in governance, the nation is poised for greater growth in the economy and is looking at joining developed nations in running an efficient, reliable and attractive stock market. It is true that not all Kenyans are equipped to handle intricacies of the market – and indeed most Africans have not even interested themselves in the glories of a stock market, but that does not mean the fruits of the labor of smarter people should not drop off the tree of success to the less fortunate. By investing in the stock market, all Kenyans win.

As we prepare to handle the next chapter, I don't want us to forget the core issue we are dealing with in this stirring discussion. The issue is the impact of elections on the stock market and how it relates to Kenyans – Africans if you please. In the next chapter, we are going to look at turbulence in the stock market. How does it affect the markets? What does it say about the state of an economy? And more importantly, how does it get corrected if a negative trend is observed?

Questions

The questions below are designed to recap key elements in this chapter. An in-depth study of issues raised in the chapter is recommended.

1. What is the role of a stock market?
2. What is:
   a. Capital?
   b. Savings?
   c. Resource management?
   d. Transparency?
3. What do the following abbreviations stand for?
   a. NSE
   b. CMA
   c. IPO
4. Discuss the impact of stability on performance of the stock market.

References

Fabozzi F. & Modigiliani F. (1995). *Capital Market Institutions and Instruments.* New Jersey: Prentice Hall, Inc.

Lee R. (1998). *What is an Exchange? The Automation, Management and Regulation of Financial Markets.* New York: Oxford University Press Inc.

http://www.nse.co.ke Nairobi Stock Exchange Website

5 Turbulence in the Stock Market

A number of studies have been undertaken establishing the relationship between the performance of stock exchanges in the world and political activities in specific countries. Most of these studies have been carried out in developed stock exchanges (Stovall 1992, Hudson et all, 1998). As one might expect, such studies lack information on emerging markets and the stock market in Kenya. What this implies is this – that investors, policymakers researchers and other critical stakeholders lack the benefits such research would have provided to them were its findings available.

The reason studies on the effect of political activities on performance of emerging capital markets is important is because more and more people are investing in these markets. Investors in these markets are locals and foreigners, with the latter becoming key players. The reason studies have to be conducted within the context of these emerging stock markets is because local and foreign investors interested in investing within them cannot rely on studies based on the developed ones. Those developed ones operate under a different:

a. **Social environment,** where most citizens already understand the value of courtesy, expectations of a culture steeped in rugged individualism, and social systems designed to cushion the weakest in the society. Such a social environment makes it easy for one to operate within a set context of expectations and understand what to give back.

b. **Economic environment,** where nations in which they operate have perfected market economics and know how to predict future trends for the sake of investing. Officials and thought-leaders mandated to make decisions on key aspects of the economy are highly trained professionals with years of experience in economic planning. Matters of monetary discipline and fiscal policy are in the hands of men vetted by the highest vetting boards in the nation. In the United States, for example, the Senate and Congress are many times given the role of vetting the Chairman of the Federal Reserve, America's central bank. In the United Kingdom, similar arrangements are in place to vet the man or woman who will oversee the activities of the Bank of England. In recent years, Kenya has adopted the policy of vetting top officials, moving away from presidential appointments that were made on the basis of cronyism and considerations other than qualification.

c. **Political environment,** where predictability is at the core of projections. In the United States and in the United Kingdom, the parties that sponsor presidential or Prime ministerial candidates are few and their policies well known. Global markets know what to expect should either a Republican or a Democrat be elected president in the United States. Similarly, markets in the United Kingdom and those around Europe will react a certain way in response to a Liberal, Tory or Conservative victory. In Kenya, it has been difficult to assess the impact on the stock market of political parties because they all sponsor men and women who are cut from the same cloth.

We need to look at graphs that reflect market volatility three months before and after elections in the critical years after Kenya's return to multiparty politics. Find them in next page:

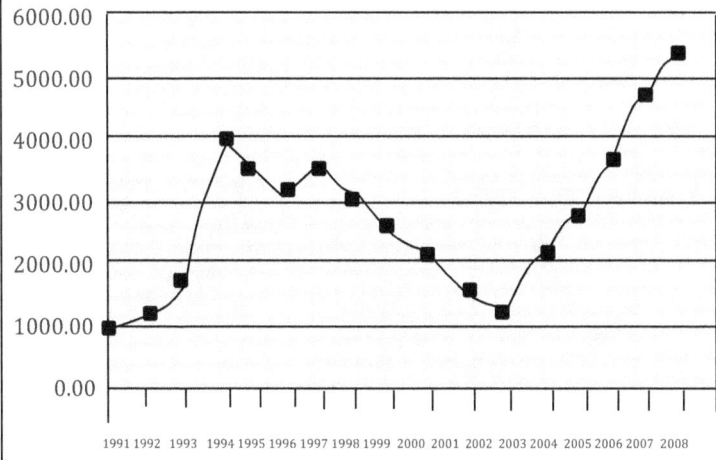

Mean NSE Index

Chart 1.5: Market Performance over study period showing trend movement

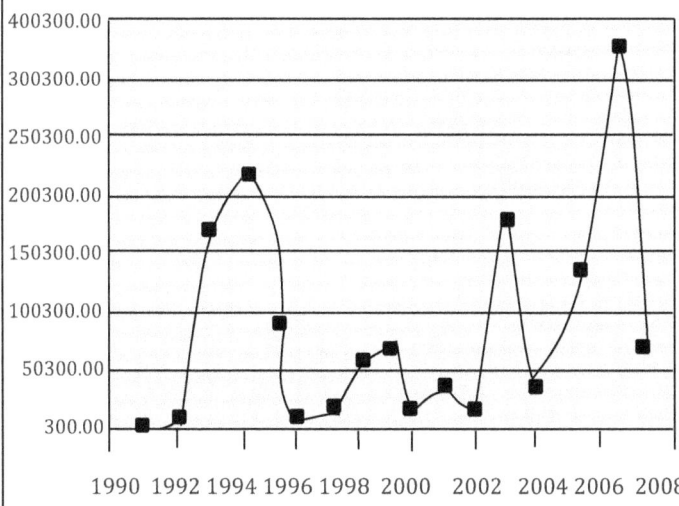

Variance

Chart 1.6: Trend movements in the market volatility over study period

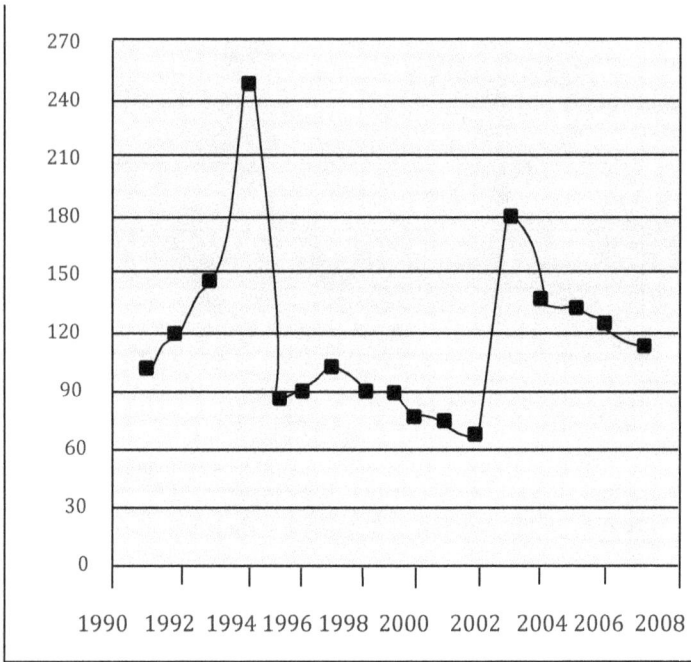

Percentage change

Chart 1.7: Trend movements of percentage change in market

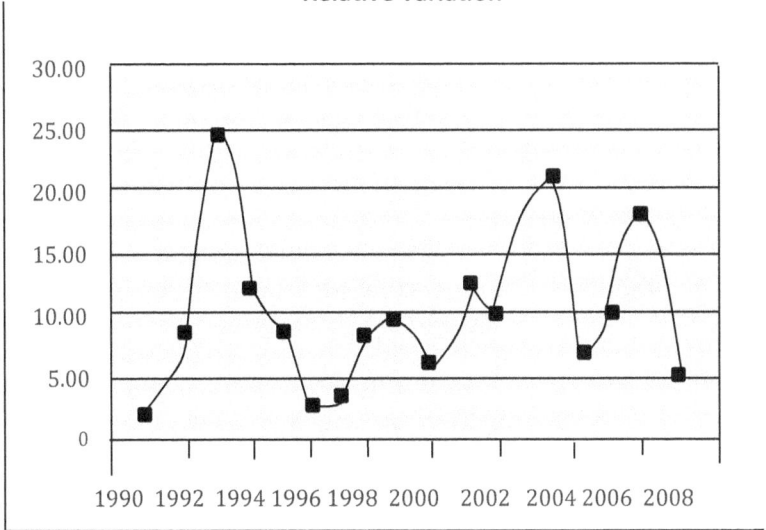

Relative variation

Chart 1.8: Trend movements of the relative market volatility

I, of course, understand that to say politicians in Kenya are all cut from the same cloth denies us the critical lenses we must wear to look at the manner a propertied rightwing in Kenya has led the nation through the post-independence years – then compare that to the blueprint Liberals or Progressives have developed.

This book is the first of its kind in discussing the nature of the Nairobi Securities Exchange before and after an election – to determine the impact of an election on the performance of Eastern Africa's largest stock market. It is probably the first comprehensive study on the impact of party politics on the stock market, but most importantly, on the quality of life of the people of Kenya. For this reason, it is necessary to understand the DNA of the forces that have been in bitter contention for political supremacy in the land.

The Conservatives

In independent Kenya, this force has been the most powerful of all the forces that have ever manifested in the land. It has been successful in retention of power, but has been a failure in using it for the benefit of all Kenyans. This force emerged and grew strong soon after Kenya gained independence from Great Britain. Led by men who had fought fiercely to send the white man away and free Kenya, the new rulers soon realized the power of land and wealth and wanted to gain both, then protect the gains by wielding unfettered power.

In the coming years, the Conservatives became wealthy and sought to use every tool at their disposal to keep power in the hands of a trusted few. Those trusted few came to be defined as men and women of immense wealth and influence. As they grew wealthier by the day, they kept other Kenyans away from the high table, where riches were divided. In essence, therefore, as this class of Kenyans became richer, the rest of Kenyans remained at the exact socio-economic spot the white man left them.

Inevitably, a desire to keep in place those structures that led them to emerge powerful and rich goaded them to work for maintenance of the status quo.

Naturally, it didn't take long before these rulers drifted away from the promise of a unified nation. The key issues that leaders vowed to tackle: poverty, illiteracy and disease fell by the wayside as acquisition of wealth became a more pressing matter. It was on the basis of that unexpected reality that Kenya Peoples Union was formed. The idea was to give Kenyans an alternative leadership platform to the increasingly drifting Kenya Africa National Union. Assessing the way Kenya has evolved since, it is fair to say it was the split of 1966 that divided the nation into fiercely competing camps that defined themselves by their core agenda.

The Status Quo Agenda

The agenda of the status quo forces included:

- **Land.** These men, having fought hard to win land back from whites, knew the value and potential of land to emerge as the most critical factor of wealth and power in Kenya. They consequently set out to acquire as much land as they could – in every part of the country. Suffice it to say that land has remained an emotive issue to date in Kenya.

- **Wealth.** The rulers also knew the value of wealth. They knew that in order to control people, one needed enormous wealth. Because of their desire to control Kenya, they set out to make money, get rich, then create wealth. There is a difference between being rich and being wealthy. Being rich is what emerging millionaires in Kenya today are. Being wealthy is what men and women who own multimillion-shilling businesses are. When a man or woman owns seven *matatus* and two *posho* mills, he or she may pass for rich, but when a man or a woman owns a giant company that supplies a certain product to the nation, owns large shares in nearly all the banks, and owns vast tracts of land, that person is no longer just rich; that person is wealthy.

- **Power.** It is not clear at what point the rulers sensed how critical power was in the emerging scheme of things, but it is clear that by 1966 they had come to the conclusion that power was such a potent tool in wealth creation and retention that they would fight to keep it in the hands of men and women who had wealth and wished to keep socio-political and economic dynamics in the new Kenyan society undisturbed.

- **Control.** You may wonder how control factors into the mind games the rulers played on Kenyans. The answer is simple, but it may be a lot more cynical than you can ever imagine. Because the rulers wanted to control Kenya, they ensured that the nation's vast resources were used only on projects that enhanced their control.

There obviously are other agenda items one could add to the status quo forces, but these were the key ones. To keep this agenda on the path to dominance, conservative forces in Kenya have coalesced around creation of wealth and the use of state power to protect it. They have come together under the guise of parties with blueprints and an ideological tilt, but when one dissects them, what remains standing is the conservatism that drives them.

The Progressives

At the other end of the political spectrum is the force we may refer to as liberal or progressive. These are the politicians and thought-leaders across Kenya who have been brought together by a desire to make the nation work for all. In the realm of Kenyan politics, they have fared poorly because they have never held the Presidency in any credible manner. It is thus fair to say that the burden of inequality Kenyans experience today is a creation of the status quo forces and their voracious appetite for land and wealth.

The Progressive Agenda

The agenda of the progressive forces included:

- **Land redistribution**. From the very beginning, those who stood for equitable distribution of the nation's resources watched with alarm as rulers hived off huge chunks of land and even forcibly evicted people in the process. The progressives didn't like this. They have fought hard to enact laws and create a situation that would allow the nation to heal by addressing this land issue. In the March 2013 election, this matter became a pivotal election issue. It is clear that Kenya will never be at peace with herself unless this aggressive land cancer is kept from spreading.
- **Wealth creation for all.** The premise is that Kenya is for all the people of Kenya and should be enjoyed by the nation's citizens.
- **Democratic Rule.** Progressives believe the only way Kenya can move forward is by embracing

democratic rule, complete with a vibrant press, a functioning legislature, an independent judiciary, a trustworthy electoral body and a military command structure that embraces Kenya.

- **Devolution.** From the very beginning, devolution has been a political option minorities have viewed as a viable alternative to a centralized structure controlled in Nairobi. Progressives, who drove the devolution agenda, reasoned that Kenyans needed to slice the nation into enclaves where each group of people could develop themselves at their own pace. In 2013, devolution became entrenched in the promulgated constitution.

- **National Healing and Unity.** Progressives believe Kenya can and must move toward the day unity of purpose will be at the core of the nation's agenda and political dialogue. For the sake of healing, they say, leaders and institutions must be deliberate about fostering an environment that cultivates peace, love and unity – as flown on the flag.

We have discussed these forces in-depth so that their core values are evident in relation to the way they affect the stock market when one or the other is in power. As we have already noted, Conservatives have held power the longest in Kenya. Through Kenya African National

Union, they ruled Kenya since independence and were only sent packing in 2002, when a mixed breed of Conservatives and Liberals ganged up to deny the ruling party KANU another chance at the helm. Fortunately for Kenyan politics, the line that divides Conservatives and Liberals is getting more defined and their agenda for the nation crystalizing into ideological isms that can be clearly identified as liberalism or conservatism.

The question we need to answer, as we look forward to the next chapter, is therefore this: why have I bothered to carry out a study on a matter most Kenyans would care less about? Why have I delved deep into murky politics to seek answers to the impact of elections on our stock market? The answer is simple. It is because the stock market reflects the growth or stagnation of the economy. It is a reflection of the journey Kenya has been on. So is this book designed for all Kenyans?

Absolutely right.

Are there specific groups of officials who need to read the book so that they can enact policies which will make Kenyans live well by attracting robust local and foreign investment? The answer is yes. We need to close this chapter by making quick mention of these groups:

a. **Academicians.** Insights drawn from this book are designed to nudge scholars to engage in further research on performance of the stock markets and factors influencing their performance.

b. **Capital Markets Authority (CMA).** The authority has an opportunity to glean information to be used to educate the general public in the dynamics of the NSE during and after elections. This will help them make better investment decisions.

c. **Nairobi Stock Exchange (NSE).** This body's many workers – especially its management – have a chance to finally understand the ebb and flow of investment during and after an election. This may help them make informed decisions on how to conduct the affairs of the NSE in the period between, before and after an election. The information may also be used to make policy proposals to the Capital Markets Authority.

d. **Stockbrokers and investment banks.** Brokers and investment bankers have an opportunity to delve into the dynamics of the NSE so they can advise their clients well on investment strategies during the electioneering period.

e. **Investors.** The need to rely on solid information about the likely performance of the NSE during elections is met in this book. The information they acquire helps determine investment decisions through the Nairobi Stock Exchange.

f. **Government.** The government is finally able to rely on researched information that may help determine the timing of privatization of state corporations through the NSE.

The critical nature of a nation's stock market in assessing the quality of life of its citizens could not have been made stronger. The entities listed above play an important role in determining the overall direction of a stock market. When these entities work in coordinated harmony, the quality of life for citizens should improve – when they work at cross-purposes, it is a pointer to a deeper malaise that must be addressed at once to restore a sense of balance.

In the next chapter, we are going to deal with the very important question of the impact of general elections on performance of a stock market. Our eyes will open about the central role elections play in determining the growth, stagnation or decline of stock markets. Is the nation politically stable? Are party leaders and flagbearers men or women the markets can trust? Are the people of a given nation happy enough to become local investors due to the existence of an environment conducive for investment? These and several other pertinent questions can only be answered when we have clear understanding of the nature, dynamics, and personalities of those who present themselves for electoral office and the party platforms they represent.

Questions

The questions below are designed to recap key elements in this chapter. An in-depth study of issues raised in the chapter is recommended.

1. Identify and discuss the conservative movement in Kenya and its impact on the stock market.
2. What is the platform of:
   a. The conservative?
   c. The liberals?
3. Who is:
   a. A local investor?
   b. A foreign investor?
4. Paint a picture of a conducive environment for investment.

References

Hudson, R., Keasey, K., and Dempsey, M. (1998). Share Prices Under Tory and Labour Governments in the UK since 1945. *Applied Financial Economics, 8: 389-400.*

Stovall, R. H. (1992). Forecasting Stock Market Performance via the Presidential Cycle. *Financial Analysts Journal, May-June 1992: 5-8.*

6 Impact of General Elections on Performance of a Stock Market

We have operated under the strong presumption that elections have an impact on the stock market, based at least on studies that have been conducted in the more developed markets abroad. The distinctive advantage these markets have is that they have operated in stable economies and have enjoyed the predictability that comes with such political and social stability. The only area they may have faced uncertainty from time to time is in the economic realm – the reason being that in a globally connected economy, seismic effects in one end of the globe will reverberate elsewhere within minutes. In Kenya, on the other hand, volatility may tend to be sharper because electoral predictability has proved elusive each time the nation faces an election.

Having delved deeply into matters of stock market dynamics and how they affect the average Kenyan in previous chapters, we now want to turn our attention to the core subject of this discussion. The question we have been seeking to answer is: do general elections have an impact on the stock market? Does it matter whether the conservatives or the liberals win an election in Kenya? What party does the Nairobi Securities Exchange prefer to see handed victory in an election? These are the critical questions we need to address by comparing our nascent market to the more developed ones.

Despite the significant appeal of the notion that political forces affect the United States stock market, there has been little systematic research examining the question. The discussion in this book has acted as, perhaps, the first comprehensive attempt at comparing our growth to that experienced by the mature stock markets of the West. We have and continue to focus on the impact of politics on the stock market in Kenya. In the United States, there are three major hypotheses that have been tested in terms of political effects on U.S. stock returns (Jones, 2002).

The first hypothesis tests the popular wisdom that over time the stock market prefers Republican presidential administrations to Democratic ones. This effect is referred to as the *party effect*. The second hypothesis – related to the first in that the subject of interest is the president's political party, tests the market's immediate reaction to the election of a Democratic or Republican president. This is called the *election reaction* effect. Then like the first two political effects, the third hypothesis rests on the popular wisdom that the last two years of a president's four-year term feature better stock performance than the first two years and consequently the third effect of interest is the second-half effect (Jones, 2002).

The question that must immediately come to mind is – do these patterns hold true in Kenya? Do we also experience the first, second and third effect in the manner the Americans do? As we already noted, Kenya has not had ideologically-grounded parties and even less of an experience with alternative leaderships because the nation has tended to be ruled by conservatives. The liberals have not had a long enough stint, though it may be argued that the coalition government of President Mwai Kibaki and Prime Minister Raila Odinga was the first left-leaning one Kenyans experienced.

Popular wisdom holds that the coalition government nurtured an atmosphere where democratic tenets created a *feel good* effect in the nation. This made the stock market rally and growth was experienced. Does this mean, though, that conservative presidencies have developed the stock market at a slower pace? To answer that question, we need to look at the manner the U.S. stock market has reacted to Democratic and Republican electoral wins – and base these on reality rather than what we have called popular wisdom.

The party effect, in which popular wisdom asserts that the stock market prefers Republican presidents to Democratic ones, turns out to be false. Indeed, evidence supports the opposite proposition in that stocks perform much better under a Democratic president than under a Republican leadership. Siegel (1998), carrying out a study on this subject matter in the period between 1888 and 1997, arrived at a conclusion that agrees with the statement that indeed Democrats are better for the stock market than Republicans.

Logically, we have to interrogate the reason stocks rally under Democrats and not Republicans. Is it based on their policies – monetary, fiscal and foreign? Democrats tend to be the men and women who are progressive and seek inclusion to the widest extent in social, economic and political life in the nation. Globally, they are the party that endeavors to work with nations around the world to tackle threats and share in the successes. Could this be the *feel good* effect the coalition government brought to Kenya between 2009 and 2012? More crucially, do liberal governments around the world operate on the same economic, domestic and foreign policy framework?

Interestingly, Johnson and Chittenden (1999) carried out a similar study on the Standard & Poors 500 Index (S&P), based on party affiliation of the president during the 1929 to 1996 period, and reported no credible change in stock performance. When the same authors used an index of small stocks, *party effect* was pronounced, with stock performing much better under Democratic presidents than Republican ones.

This question of differential returns by political party has also been tested in England by Hudson, Keasey and Dempsey (1998). These three researchers found no difference in the performance of the Financial Times 30 Share Index between Tory and Labour governments. Could these findings signal a more mature market that is not swayed by elections because fiscal and monetary policies are not affected by power politics?

Studies using various event methodologies have provided consistent evidence that the immediate market reaction to the election of a Republican president is a positive one while the election of a Democratic president creates a negative market reaction. Siegel (1998) found out that from 1888 to 1996, the election of a republican president produced a positive market reaction as measured by the change in the Dow Jones Industrial Average, while the election of a Democrat produced a negative market reaction. Two other studies of broad equity markets found similar results during the period from 1900 to 1976 (Riley and Luksetich, 1980) and 1900-1968 (Niederhoffer, Gibbs, and Bullock, 1970).

Further, an event study that focused on defense industry stocks found positive excess returns in those equities when Republican presidents were elected and negative excess returns when democratic presidents were elected (Homaifar, Randolph, Helms, and Haddad, 1988). In the near-term, therefore, empirical evidence surrounding the election reaction effect is entirely consistent with popular wisdom. Like the other two effects, previous evidence supporting the second-half effect is quite consistent.

Stovall (1992) examined percentage annual change in the Dow Jones Industrial Average and found that equities performed best in the last two years of a president's term. Siegel (1998) later confirmed the second-half effect for the 1888 to 1997 period – and he noted that the third year of any president's term produced the best stock returns of the four years. Among other things, this could mean the market is anticipating change in a little over a year because campaigns are just getting underway in the third year of a presidency.

General elections are a significant driver of stocks since stock markets anticipate change. The inhibitions and misgivings traders may have had about the monetary, fiscal and foreign policy of a certain president begin to give way to enthusiasm because the end of that administration is anticipated. On the other hand, if an administration has had a net positive impact on the market, its anticipated end may spur growth as investors try to cash in ahead of the end of that administration.

In Kenya, as is the case in most of Africa, foreign policy is predictably pro-West. Because America has emerged as the sole superpower in the world, most nations on the continent of Africa follow the dictates of the United States and have been beneficiaries of that nation's support in infrastructure, innovation and other spheres. In recent years, however, there has been a shift in loyalties with some African nations being courted by a newly-assertive China. The problem for Kenya endures in the area of monetary and fiscal policy – but more significantly in the area of election management. Since the glorious return of multiparty politics, the nation has approached each new election with fear and trembling because raw ethnic passions are stirred by unscrupulous politicians to cause tension for their own advantage.

Market volatility is, thus, a permanent problem the NSE faces whenever an election season sets in. Unlike in the United States and Great Britain, where outcomes have no significant impact on the market, in Kenya outcomes can precipitate panic buying or sudden dumping based on assessment of the person elected president. This is as a result of the fact that most Kenyan parties, and the men or women they nominate as flagbearers, lack solid commitment to a cohesive set of ideas that will be followed once in office. The lack of predictability these politicians bring to office is problematic for the market. Indeed, there are observers who have said, of the African elections, that the only predictable outcome about them is that they are unpredictable!

The second-half effect is even more unpredictable in Africa. On a continent where there is no guarantee a losing incumbent will leave office peacefully, the best a stock market can anticipate is trouble. Recent events in Burundi have served to amplify this point – because the president has refused to step aside in spite of his two-term stint coming to an end. The ease with which African strongmen manipulate constitutions to extend terms in office and run the risk of precipitating political upheavals is a matter for which a solution needs to be found. It is in nations where democratic tenets are not honored that we have to wonder why a stock market should exist at all.

In a study of monthly prices the Standard & Poors 400 between 1948 and 1978, Allvine and Oneill (1980) also observed that the last two years of the four-year term produced better stock returns than did the first two years. Similar results are reported by Huang (1985), for the 1929 to 1996 period, and by Johnson and Chittenden (1999), for the 1929 to 1996 period. Contrast that to the situation in Burundi, where a year or more will be lost as the president battles to stabilize his government. How will stocks in Bujumbura fare in that situation?

In Kenya, the economy experienced the worst period ever and growth stagnated after the tremors of post-election violence in 2007-2008. In the stunning orgy of death and bloodletting that followed the hotly disputed election, confidence in the nation's ability to run free and fair elections plummeted as the world watched in horror events in the East African powerhouse. Over the next two to three years, the coalition government put in place measures to restore confidence in foreign capitals about Kenya's ability to run her affairs, but as one may imagine, two years were lost, denying the market the second-half effect, and by the time the nation faced another election, memories of the last took center-stage, making the mood at the Nairobi Securities Exchange dampen.

Could it be fair to say, therefore, that most African stock markets fare better in the middle of a president's term than follow the patterns observed in Western markets? The answer to this question must be a tentative yes – because growth in such markets would be pegged on a number of issues:

a. **Political stability**. This can only be created in an environment where peace has finally prevailed after an election. In most of Africa, peace may follow a long period of instability and death, but when it eventually comes, markets are capable of starting a slow journey back to profitability. This inevitably raises the question of whether, so far, elective politics has served Africa well or not.

b. **Fiscal discipline**. In many African nations, leaders have found it hard to separate a nation's money from their private money. In Uganda, there once was a president who knew nothing about fiscal discipline and famously asked his treasury team to print more money if there was no money, as they had reported to him. There has been a trend where better educated men become leaders in

Africa, but cases still abound where the actions of the educated and the ignorant mirror each other.

c. **Foreign relations**. We already pointed out that Africa leans West in foreign relations, but China has lately come in to offer an alternative voice. A nation that will prosper must engage all nations in trade and join the military and economic blocs within her region. In Africa, there is ECOWAS, IGAD and COMESA. These are bodies that should help a nation steer its stock market and economy to greater heights if they are interacted with innovatively and with the sole aim of making the life of citizens better.

d. **Predictability**. The political environment is changing fast in Africa, but there was a time when the only predictable governments were those run by brutal, efficient dictators. In the case of a benevolent dictatorship, which many observers believe is what runs Rwanda today, stocks would rally because the nation was in stable hands and the projection was that nothing would change any time soon. That sorry state of predictability at the expense of democracy served the stock market well, as it probably has in Kigali, but it undermines growth toward the emergence of a democratic, nation, vibrant nation. So, is this the nature of predictability Africa should be proud of?

Despite the empirical support for the popular wisdom that the last two years of the presidential cycle are better for stocks than are the first two years in the United States, the same effect apparently does not apply to England, where one study reported no difference at all in stock returns over the terms of the various British governments (Hudson et al., 1998). The only popular wisdom in Africa remains one where each ethnic group will predictably vote for a man from that community. With the exception of Tanzania, where *Ujamma* or socialism seems to have unified the people, other nations wallow in negative ethnicity and are always moments away from implosion.

Civilian coups – the new trend

In the last couple of years, observers have noted that a new trend has taken root in Africa, where civilians run for election but are backed heavily by military top brass. There have been claims in various nations that the military is always responsible for the man or woman selected to lead – which is the man or woman who will be "elected" by the people as silently demanded by the men in uniform. The idea is to achieve certain critical goals that work for the elite class in a nation.

a. **Status quo**. Over the years, an elite class of citizens has emerged in all African nations. This is a class of wealthy, powerful tycoons who want to see nothing but peace prevail so that continued patronage of state resources is assured.

b. **Stability**. In the absence of stability, this class of elite Africans is in danger. Because they are the ones normally associated with theft, murder and other ills, an unstable nation – which might force them to flee into unpredictable exile – is the last thing they want. It was for people like them that the policy of order at all cost was invented.

c. **Superclass**. This is a situation where rulers have decided that they belong to a class more superior to ordinary citizens. Members of the superclass are drawn from top political leaders, leading corporate chiefs, high-level military brass and top church officials. Because it is the military that is authorized to legally carry and use weapons, this superclass relies on it to be the doorkeeper – to prevent ordinary men and women from joining the group. It is no wonder, therefore, that most children of the elite find it easy to mingle at a time many Africans butcher one another in the hope of putting their man in the State House. Voters must be aware that the superclass in Africa will always worry about themselves first, then act on the needs of others later. What the Americans call trickledown economics is what they practice – so that leftovers are the best the common man can hope for.

A civilian coup is, therefore, a military takeover where a civilian is placed at the command apex. It is a situation where a president is "elected" in name only, because when it comes right down to it, such a man or woman is just but an instrument of the superclass and is tasked to do nothing else except maintain the status quo. Radical shifts that may bring in a charismatic commoner are not anticipated in this scheme of things – the only virtue is the firm lid to be placed on commoners so that they are fed the illusion of progress and peace.

Party effect on the Nairobi Securities Exchange

We have labored under the assumption that elections have an impact on stock performance. In Africa, though, we have established that the dynamics at play may not necessarily follow neat patterns observed in the more developed stock markets abroad. Indeed, in Kenya, for example, parties have been formed and their manifestos made public, but there have been only two movements to mean anything in Kenya politics – these have been the conservative and liberal movement. So then, which of the two is better for the stock market?

In the United States, as in other nations around the world, Democrats or liberals tend to have policies that create the *feel good* effect and cause a rise in stocks markets. This is because they abide more closely by the tenets of democracy and fight for inclusion rather than exclusion. In a democratic environment, a couple of factors are to be expected, which contribute to the feel good effect:

a. **A democratically-elected President**. This is a president for whom nothing can be said that his election was rigged. In many instances, democrats prefer clear victories that confer legitimacy on them. With that legitimacy, they find it easy to execute their mandate as they work to strengthen the policies of inclusion, vibrant foreign relations, fiscal discipline and progressivism in all areas.

b. **A vibrant Press**. The press in Africa has been accused of acting at the behest of the power elite. In most instances, it has been seen to report only news favorable to the leaders and to ignore the Opposition. In a democratic or liberal government, the press is accorded the space it needs to carry out investigations, write critical editorials and play its role of thought-leadership without the fear of facing victimization.

c. **An independent Judiciary**. Two critical factors have undermined independence of the judiciary in Africa:

- Corruption, which compromises judicial officers in the administration of justice as they accept bribes and bend justice to favor those who have bribed them.
- Intimidation, which happens when state officials coarse and threaten a magistrate or judge with firing, denial of benefits or even death.

A democratic government is one in which judicial officers feel safe and protected by immutable guarantees within the law books regarding their security – as long as they act within the laid down framework of their duties.

d. **A functioning Legislature**. Kenya – and several other nations across Africa – has endured years of a Legislature tilted in favor of the Executive, thus acting more as a rubberstamp for the decisions already made at State House rather than a body where laws are vigorously debated, interrogated then made. In a democratic administration, the Legislature must be accorded space to act only in a manner that is consistent with its call.

e. **A Military in the barracks**. In the years gone by, coups were an ever present danger all across the continent of Africa. Military generals were in the despicable habit of kicking out lawful presidents by organizing coups. In a democratic government, the military must remain in the barracks and act only to protect the territorial integrity of a nation; not to subjugate and harass citizens.

Without a doubt, the movements around the world that foster an atmosphere where these core democratic tenets abound are liberal – not conservative movements. Like the Democrats in the United States, the Liberals in Africa are better placed to enact policies that would create the feel good effect by living up to fiscal discipline, a domestic policy that is all inclusive and a foreign policy that respects other nations and builds bridges.

So, should Kenyans vote in only Liberal administrations each election cycle? The role of this book is to discuss the impact of elections on the stock market, and the impact of the stock market on the quality of life. It is, therefore, wise that having come this far, we also look at a historical perspective of the general elections in Kenya. In the next chapter, we want to look at how political parties fared on in past elections and how their policies affected the stock market – and thus the quality of life of Kenyans.

Questions

The questions below are designed to recap key elements in this chapter. An in-depth study of issues raised in the chapter is recommended.

1. Name and discuss the three major hypotheses that have been tested in terms of political effects on U.S. stock returns.
2. What is:
   a. Party effect?
   b. Election reaction effect?
   c. Second-half effect?
   d. Feel good effect?
3. Discuss the impact of foreign policy on a nation's stock performance.
4. What does it mean to be pro-West?
5. Define a civilian coup.

References

Allvine, F. C. and O'Neill, D. E. (1980). Stock Market Returns and the Presidential Election Cycle. *Financial Analysts Journal, September-October: 49-56.*

Homaifar, G., Randolph, W., Helms, B. P., and Haddad, M. (1988). American Presidential Elections and Returns of Defense Industry Stocks. *Applied Economics, 20: 985-993.*

Huang, R. D. (1985). Common Stock Returns and Presidential Elections. *Financial Analysts Journal, March-April: 58-61.*

Hudson, R., Keasey, K., and Dempsey, M. (1998). Share Prices Under Tory and Labour Governments in the UK since 1945. *Applied Financial Economics, 8: 389-400.*

Jones, T. (2002). Presidential Election Cycles and Stock Market Returns. *Conference Paper for the American Academy and Finance.* New York: McGraw Hill.

Niederhoffer, V., Gibbs, S., and Bullock, J. (1970). Presidential Elections and the Stock Market. *Financial Analysts Journal, March-April: 111-113.*

Riley, F. & W. B. and Luksetich, W. A. (1980). The Market Prefers Republicans: Myth or Reality. *Journal of Financial and Quantitative Analysis, 15 (3): 541-560.*

Stovall, R. H. (1992). Forecasting Stock Market Performance via the Presidential Cycle. *Financial Analysts Journal, May-June 1992: 5-8.*

Siegel, J. J. (1998). *Stocks for the Long Run.* New York: McGraw Hill.

http://www.nse.co.ke Nairobi Stock Exchange Website

7 Historical Perspective of General Elections in Kenya

The place to start, as we discuss Kenya's brief history of elections, is the beginning. In the days of colonial rule, the natives were not allowed to vote and indeed, there was no voting of any nature in the country – leaders were appointed by authorities in London. The appointed white leaders later appointed chiefs and other low level folks in the villages to watch over the people. As Kenya prepared for independence, two competing national parties were formed: Kenya African National Union (KANU) and Kenya African Democratic Union (KADU). After their formation, two pre-independence elections took place and KANU won both, probably a pointer to the dominance it would enjoy in Kenyan politics in the years to come.

On 12th December, 1963, Kenya achieved independence from the Great Britain and a year later, the Republic of Kenya was born (http://africanelections.tripod.com/ke). Since that early beginning, the nation has carried out a number of elections, many of which appeared hopelessly flawed, some rigged and others violently contested, but when one places Kenya side-by-side with other African nations, it is fair to say the nation has come through the labyrinth of electoral politics far better than others. Our moments of grimness have been trapped between many moments of glory and skirmishes have been confined to certain parts of the country, not as widespread as media reports sometimes paint them to be.

The first President of the Republic of Kenya died in office in 1978 and was constitutionally succeeded by his Vice President. During the administration of the nation's second President, there was a coup attempt, which led the Head of State and his handlers to declare Kenya a de jure one party state. This was ratified by the rubber stamp National Assembly in June 1982.

Following that development, Kenya plunged into the days of dictatorial darkness. All the institutions that supported democratic governance were systematically destroyed as the nation descended into a police state in every manner but name. Opposition politicians were hounded and locked up, the press was muzzled and many reporters jailed, leading clergymen were threatened with dire consequences for their provocative sermons, and an unprecedented atmosphere of fear took root in Kenya.

The NSE Prophecy

Those ten years of autocratic rule came to an end in December 1991, when the ruling party KANU convened a special conference and returned Kenya to the glory of multiparty politics, opening the way for legal registration of parties and change in the constitution to limit the term limit of a president to two five-year terms. By the time this decision was reached, KANU had endured years of agitation for greater freedoms and many people had been killed in the process. Those were the gravely uncertain days when the stock market stumbled and danced to the unpredictability of a government devoid of a unifying agenda for Kenya. KANU grudgingly returned Kenya to multiparty politics, but not without a stern warning – that many parties would fracture the nation along ethnic lines. This is a prophecy that may have come true. We are still discussing the impact of general elections on the stock market. Because of Kenya's return to multiparty politics in 1991, it makes sense to start our discussion of the nature of the elections that took place after that fact. The first one took place in 1992.

The 1992 General Election

As we have already discussed, this election was the first of its kind in Kenya because the nation had just returned to competitive politics. There were a total of eight parties that contested (NEMU, 1992). In what observers viewed as flawed polls, KANU went on to win a comfortably majority in Parliament and the incumbent was reelected.

As historians look back at that period, records will show that tribal skirmishes in the vast Rift Valley and other hotspots across Kenya clouded the atmosphere and made it difficult for the nation to hold free and fair elections. There were claims of intimidation, rigging, and threats as people went to the ballot – all factors that played a role in giving the ruling party a wide margin at the polls. The stock market reacted to these events by maintaining slow growth and many feared it had become sick.

With KANU back in power, Kenya started a long journey to the future. The government walked away from sound fiscal and monetary policies and raffled feathers with all key international allies, causing the nation's economy to teeter on the brink of collapse. Key among the issue that KANU turned a blind eye to were:

a. **Nepotism**. This was a cancer that weaved its way through the fabric of the nation and caused the government to preside over an administration of relatives and friends and cronies. Credentials and qualifications and experience ceased to matter as long as one had the right name and pedigree.

b. **Fiscal indiscipline**. This was another cancer that Kenya had to grapple with as it appeared those in power turned a blind eye to the gross misuse of public funds. The Central Bank of Kenya failed to play its mandated role of ensuring adherence to budgets and projections laid out in the national budget. Indiscipline shot through the roof.

c. **Growing pariah status**. Within the community of nations, Kenya was fast becoming a young nation regarded as failing or failed already, but tough-talking officials in Nairobi didn't seem to care. They accused friendly Western powers of seeking to colonialize Kenya afresh – something they knew the Westerners shrunk when they heard. This hard approach earned Kenya enemies rather than friends and gravely affected the stock market.

d. **Growing police state**. Observers have made the point that KANU's repressive ways started shortly after the 1982 coup – and that may be the case – but what followed was a deliberate remaking of Kenya into totalitarian state where the police were everywhere and listened to conversations and arrested perceived opponents of the state.

e. **Rise of military**. It was during KANU's leadership that the mix of civilian-military rule started. The military has since become a key player in elections by supporting an establishment candidate, which usually means a candidate preferred by status quo elite in the nation.

In 1997, there were fifteen presidential candidates as compared to seven candidates in 1992. This time, though, KANU won a slimmer majority in Parliament, perhaps a pointer to the fact that Kenyans were getting fed up with KANU's repressive rule. The incumbent president won that election, but based on his future behavior, it was clear he learnt a lesson from his diminishing majority in Parliament. He read well the message of Kenyans and, perhaps, started laying a solid framework for one day turning over power peacefully to whoever won it. He was being pragmatic (http://africanelections.tripod.com/ke).

The 2002 General Election

The 2002 general election was a watershed event in the history of Kenya. It has been viewed as a transitional general election because it became the first time KANU was defeated and a competitively elected president took office. Because of the unity of the Opposition, as Kenyans trooped to the polls, the incumbent party KANU, and its preferred candidate, was soundly beaten, making Kenyans believe they finally had a chance to make systems and institutions in the nation work again.

The stock market reacted to optimism in the nation by rallying. It was helped, in part, by the fact that the newly-elected president was a trained economist – a graduate of the London School of Economics.

In the years that followed, Kenya's image abroad had a makeover as the government embarked on international relations, fiscal discipline, sound monetary policies and a credible effort at unifying the nation. There are those who believe that the National Rainbow Coalition (NARC) government became the first to govern from center-left rather than center-right like the ones that had gone before it. Its bold manifesto was broadly a mirror of the Democratic Party's in the United States, but made to suit the peculiar needs of the people of Kenya.

Five candidates contested this election, which was held on December 27, 2002, but most of them offered only token opposition to the juggernaut built by Kenya's top parties under the Rainbow Coalition. When results were later announced, the Head of State gracefully conceded defeat and saved Kenya from possible turmoil. It was a peaceful transfer of power that made markets already in the bull zone continued to soar as optimism abounded in all corners of Kenya (Commonwealth, 2006).

By this time, even those who hadn't understood the dynamics of a stock market to respond positively to free and fair general elections must have taken note of the bull market. There, clearly, was an observable correlation between gains in the stock market and peaceful, credible elections. The market loved positive news, a situation where predictability and peace abounded and growth was made certain by the promise of fiscal discipline and sound monetary policies. Of course, it didn't hurt at all that the nation was finally in the hands of a leader who got elected popularly – by all ethnic hues in the country.

The promise of the Rainbow Coalition was, however, cut short when disagreements set in and key partners in the movement went their separate ways. The stock market experienced a dumper, but the total sense of negativity that once was pervasive didn't return. Because of those disagreements, Kenya went into the 2007 election as a nation unified in hope, but secretly at war with itself.

The 2007 General Election

The election held on December 27, 2007, was the most competitive in the nation's history – with a record nine presidential candidates. The voting process proceeded smoothly and vote tallying went well, but matters turned nasty when results were late in being announced, causing heightening tension across the land. Observers of the stock market at that time noticed a corresponding rise in tension at the market as Kenya became gloomier with each passing day of delayed results.

On December 30th, 2007, the Electoral Commission of Kenya (ECK) announced the incumbent as the winner and he was sworn in the same day for a second term. ODM promptly rejected those results and what followed was violence on an unprecedented scale in the nation, especially in the Opposition strongholds, as aggrieved leaders rejected those results (Commonwealth, 2008).

What started as mere protests later turned into a season of bloodletting and destruction of property on a scale Kenya had never witnessed. The market literally crashed in what became a time of shame for Kenya. Afraid to face another prospect of a Rwanda in Kenya, the international community rallied and forced antagonists to the table of negotiations. Led by Secretary-General Kofi Annan and a team of eminent personalities in Africa, it took several days to achieve a breakthrough – as killings and wanton destruction of property went on unabated.

As dust later settled, a Coalition Government was formed and Kenya woke up to the reality that the economy had been badly shaken by the violence. The stock market was closed for so many days that upon its reopening, it took long for it to regain its old footing. The mood in the nation remained gloomy as people took stock of the losses and assessed the burden of starting over. But by far, the most ominous matter was the ethnic passions the violence occasioned. How was the Coalition Government going to restore the agenda of unity in such a deeply fractured nation? How were people going to work as one when grim stories of neighbor rising against neighbor on account of ethnicity were now all over the place? Such were the stakes as leaders got down to business.

Through focus and hard work, the Coalition Government turned around the situation and by the end of its term in 2013, the nation had returned to unity of purpose. The stock market made tremendous gains and the future looked so bright that as he left office, the Head of State made the declaration that he had created an environment for Kenya's economic takeoff. Lingering memories of the 2007 violence, however, marred performance of the stocks as people didn't know what to expect.

The 2013 General Election

The Coalition Government ended on a positive note and gave way to another competitive election in 2013. This election ended up with a dispute, but it was resolved by the Supreme Court of Kenya. After its resolution, stocks have risen and Kenya has taken her place as a pivotal regional power – a leader in communication, trade and other areas of business in Eastern and central Africa.

The next election will be held in 2017. It will be followed by future elections. The lessons of the stock market are threefold – as we have already established:

a. The stock market responds well to a government headed by men and women who adhere to solid democratic rule. Free and fair elections, followed by fiscal discipline, sound monetary policies and engagement with global partners, is key to growth and participation in a global economy.

b. The stock market loves peace and predictability. Whenever elections are divisive and the tone too ethnic, the market shrinks; whenever elections are uplifting and the tone positive, stocks rise. Peace and predictability are two critical elements in any nation that wishes to build a strong stock market.

The stock market is a credible indicator of trends in a given nation – social, political and economic. Investors are always keen on events and have their ear on the ground about the present and the future. When a stock market starts to shrink, it should be a warning for leaders to take corrective measures to restore stability. Those measures may need to be taken in politics, the economy or even in a matter of social significance. The point is – the stock market's warning should be heeded.

c. The stock market is an indicator of the quality of life a nation is giving its people. A nation that has a great stock market will be one that has money to innovatively generate a high quality of life for its citizens. A nation that has a primitive stock market will be one that wallows in all the negative trends: political instability, fiscal indiscipline, and waring the label of a pariah state. A nation like that will not have money to build a solid foundation for a high quality of life for its citizens. A great stock market, therefore, is a reliable indicator of good governance.

There is no doubt that elections have a great impact on the stock market and quality of life of citizens. In the more developed nations, candidates and the parties they represent are witheringly interviewed and their views interrogated so that a measure of predictability is established. Kenya is rapidly coming to the point where the press and other systems tasked to assess the nature of leaders will do what the West does. As demonstrated by the numerous rises and falls in the Nairobi Securities

Exchange, Kenya has achieved a lot and the nation is on a promising path to modernity, but key challenges remain and those are the ones to worry about as the nation rallies to secure her future.

Questions

The questions below are designed to recap key elements in this chapter. An in-depth study of issues raised in the chapter is recommended.

1. Define *de jure* one party state.
2. What is:
    a. Nepotism?
    b. Pariah state?
    c. Police state?
3. What is the constitutional role of the Independent Electoral Boundaries Commission (IEBC)?
4. How did the 2007/2008 post-election violence affect the Nairobi Stock Market?

References

Commonwealth. (2006). *The Report of the 2002 Kenya General Election Common Wealth Observer Group.*

National Election Monitoring Unit (NEMU) 1992 General Election.

http://www.africanelections.tripod.com/ke – African Election Database website

8 The Place of God in Stocks

The question we want to answer in this chapter is: does God have a role to play in the security and prosperity of a nation? Does the Nairobi Securities Exchange retain the capacity to respond to the silent voice of divine guidance? In order to have a clear understanding of this deep matter, we have to begin by exploring leadership.

Leadership

There are many books that have been written on the subject of leadership, but most or all of them have missed the point when it comes to the core matter because they have failed to place God at the center of things. The fresh thought I bring to the discussion on leadership is this: there is only one force in the universe that is the originator, sustainer and provider for all life under the sun. That force is God. Because of His creative role, He alone is the leader the universe has ever had.

What that means is something profound – *that all leaders in the world, in whatever sphere of influence they are, only borrow an aspect of leadership from the only leader there is.* This is the revelation Flavius Josephus received many years ago, and is also the revelation most of the political, corporate, religious and military leaders in Africa – and many around the world – have not received or have deliberately denied in a misguided quest for greatness.

To be a leader, under God's divine plan, there are key elements that have to be considered:

a. **A call**. A nation will only proper when the person that occupies the highest office in the land is a man or a woman the Lord has called and inspired to lead His people. A person like that will have his or her priorities aligned to God's agenda of salvation and will lead the people toward a fulfilment of that purpose.

a. **A vision**. A leader is not a man or woman who will issue orders and wield a club to beat people back to shape, but one who will inspire people to follow him or her as his or her will is surrendered to God's wise leadership. Such a leader's vision will be shaped by divine schemes and the people will prosper because the Lord has nothing but a desire to make His people prosper and worship Him.

b. **Humility**. Great leadership is bestowed solely upon those who are humble enough to understand that their source of wisdom and strength is God. A nation whose leader is a man or woman with humility is a nation that will prosper and its stock market will reflect constant growth – because the real leader is God.

Because we are dealing, in this chapter, with matters divine, it is important that we also discuss the other realm. Just as there will be men and women who draw their inspiration from the great leadership of God, there will be others who draw theirs from Satan and offer sacrifices aimed at placating the thirty desires of demonic forces in order to stay in power. Woe unto a nation whose leaders depend on these evil forces because the nations will inevitably succumb to bloodshed, destruction and pain – because the devil comes to kill and destroy.

Given the ferocious fight for control of the hearts and minds of people in the universe between good and evil, it is critical for Kenyans – and citizens across the world, to realize that the quality of life they live will be directly affected by the nature of man or woman they elect to lead them. The storehouse of heaven is only open to those who prayerfully seek God's guidance and protection over His people through them. A leader whose heart is connected to God will thus bless his or her people by keeping the nation focused on God's supremacy.

So does it matter whether one is a Conservative or a Liberal in Kenya? Does it matter whether one is a Democrat or a republican in the United States? Does it matter whether one is in the Likud Party or Labor in Israel? Indeed it matters, but it matters even more to which force that leader aligns the agenda of his or her nation. Alignment with the forces of evil will orchestrate instant glory and moments of quick, but deceptive prosperity in a nation – there will be nothing lasting. Alignment with the forces of God will create an atmosphere of calm assurance and days of prosperity built on the firm foundation of a God who offers love eternal. If you have ever wondered why certain political leaders are so critical of religious leaders who warn of a wrong path when a nation is sliding into immoral and unethical behavior, there you have it. It is because they have their leadership aligned to evil and would rather not hear the voice of God.

The stock market in a nation led by godly men and women will show a steady rise because the protective shield of God's favor will rest on that nation. The *feel good* effect that causes markets to rise and their performance to remain steady will triple in such a nation because any time a nation walks in the precepts of God citizens can feel it – and they love it. So, should the people of Africa elect only men and women who are godly? Should being a good Christian be a requirement for leadership?

Because of my conviction on this matter – and because of my love for Africa – I will not give you a politically correct answer to this important question. The answer is **yes**. The time has come for Africa to elect men and women who love the Lord and are ready to be guided *only* by Him. Such men and women will inevitably be democratic, kind and humble. The nations will prosper under them because the storehouse of heaven will be open to the people as they pray each morning for favor from the halls of the State house.

This also explains why nations that insult God's people are trapped in endemic poverty. It is because their leaders have failed to realize that there is a formula to leadership for nations that prosper. In such nations, the President and other political leaders have a key partner in their work – a man of God. While the President prays for wisdom and favor on his people from the hills of the

State House, the man of God will be praying from the temple, church or cathedral for the President and the nation. And when the two are seen to be working together, a nation's feel good effect soars, resulting in a bullish market and high quality of life for the people.

In a pure theocracy, the civil leader is believed to have a personal connection with the civilization's religion or belief. For example, Moses led the Israelites and kept them focused on God. Law proclaimed by the ruler is considered a divine revelation, and hence the law of God. An ecclesiocracy, on the other hand, is a situation where religious leaders assume a leading role in the state, but do not claim that they are instruments of divine revelation.

A state run on the hybrid basis of an ecclesiocracy may use the administrative hierarchy of the religion for its administration, or it may have two arms – administrators and clergy – with the state's administrative hierarchy subordinate to the religious hierarchy. I have explained this unique mix to demonstrate what Africa does not need. Africa does not need a religious zealot who will exploit religion to perpetuate him or herself in power. The continent does not need a hybrid of the nature I have just described because unscrupulous leaders will exploit it by claiming *God is on our side* as they institute actions contrary to biblical or constitutional precepts. *What Africa needs is a democratic government led by a man or woman who is a servant of the Most High God.* A government like that is neither a theocracy, an ecclesiocracy nor democracy – it is a government led by divine inspiration for the sake of God's people. That is what Africa has always needed and is what she needs today!

The cure for Africa's ills

There will be those who read this chapter and shake their heads in disbelief, wondering how a scholar of my credibility can reduce Africa's ills to lack of God's reign in the hearts of the continent's leaders. They will say that I have forgotten the conspiratorial global forces that have acted to keep Africa poor and irrelevant; that I have forgotten the forces of nature that have showered on Africa famine, floods and epidemics; that I have forgotten the tricky ethnic powder keg that has turned the continent into a wasteland of civil wars.

They will be wrong.

Mine is the lonely voice of an accountant who has studied trends around the world and come to the realization that Africa's time for greatness has come, but the spirit of favor for greatness will only be unleashed when Africans place God at the center of national discourse by electing men and women who understand the role of God in the leadership of a nation. The continent has experienced far too many wars, diseases and poverty because prayer at the State House is limited and lacks meaning – and prayers at church are just as selfish.

Economists will prescribe tested ideas like monetary and fiscal discipline; they will urge African nations to align with the West in the global market place. I will prescribe those too. But I will go a step further. That step is to prescribe to all of Africa's ills the surest cure of all, one that will solve the continents problems and set her on a path to lasting prosperity. I prescribe God. I give Africa the Great Jehovah who alone can cure the endemic problems that have caused stock markets around the continent to stagnate, experience sluggish growth and sometimes collapse in the middle of endless pogroms.

I laud the latest developments I have observed at the stock market, including introduction of the Central Depository and Settlement Authority (CDSA) and the Automated Trading System (ATS), but while we make the stock market more modern and user-friendly, we have to remain alert to the fact that the giver of true wealth and watchman over our prosperity is the one and only leader the universe has ever had – the Lord God almighty!

The NSE Prophecy

Questions

The questions below are designed to recap key elements in this chapter. An in-depth study of issues raised in the chapter is recommended.

1. Define:
    a. Monarchy
    b. Oligarchy
    c. Democracy
    d. Theocracy
    e. Ecclesiocracy.
2. What is:
    a. A call?
    d. A vision?
    e. Humility?
3. Discuss the contention that there is a cure for all of Africa's ills.
4. What is the sole purpose for wealth creation and a bullish market?

References

www.Wikipedia.com

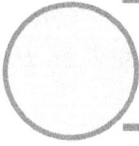

Epilogue

I have written this book with the keen sense of a son of Africa who wishes to see African nations prosper. The century for Africa's greatness has come, but we can only tap into the great wealth God has in store for us if we invite Him to sit at the table of decision-making, where corporate deals and strategies are made. He has to be the leader in all our actions by inspiring our thoughts and breathing life to them.

Ultimately, the sole purpose for wealth creation and a bullish market is the glory of God by touching the lives of the less fortunate among us with His love. As we gear up to place Africa on the global stage as God's favored land, we have to remember that one of the reasons poverty has remained in Africa for so long is lack of thanksgiving. We have failed to thank God for the minerals in the Congo and South Africa, the fertile lands of West Africa and the warm land of the Kalahari and Sahara. If we can't give thanks for the small favors, how will He bless us with bigger ones?

The stock market is the ultimate assessor of the direction a nation has taken – negative or positive. Africa's markets have been weak and many have not even taken off yet. I look to the future with optimism, however, because I believe the people of this continent will react to the sentiments expressed in this candid book by embracing the call to elect men and women who the Lord will use to uplift rather than crash our dreams.

The writers of the Kenyan National Anthem understood the place of God in the nation and wanted us to offer a prayer each time we sang the Anthem. My prayer for Kenya and Africa is based on this powerful prayer.

Kenya National Anthem

O God of all creation
Bless this our land and nation
Justice be our shield and defender
May we dwell in unity
Peace and liberty
Plenty be found within our borders

Index

Other Great Books By
Sahel Publishing Association

1. *Judy's World*, by Dr. Nicholas Letting
2. *The Doctrine of Strategic Planning*, by Dr. Edward Odundo
3. *Beyond The Rising Tide*, by Nelly Opiyo
4. *The Last Teardrop,* by Madam Lois Mbugua
5. *The Guy Who Fired His Boss*, by Sam Kariuki
6. *Understanding Arthritis*, by Dr. Omondi Oyoo
7. *The Dance Party,* by K.B. Onyango
8. *Unleash Your Full Potential,* by Sir George Wachiuri
9. *Heal Our Land,* by Sam Okello
10. *Raising A Healthy Child,* by Petronila Muthoni Agwata
11. *Soaring Like An Eagle,* by George Wachiuri
12. *Luo Kitgi Gi Timbegi E Ngima Masani,* by PLO Lumumba

And more…

There will be many more books that will answer life's toughest questions for you, because as we always say, Sahel Publishing Association's promise is: Books that speak to your hopes and fears. Call us today**: 0715.596.106**. Talk to one of Africa's most-sought ghostwriters and editors, Hon Sam Okello, about your writing dreams!

Visit any of our authors at: www.amazon.com
Our website: www.sahelpublishing.net
We are in Kenya, the U.S.A., The U.K. and India
Publish your book with us today!

www.ingramcontent.com/pod-product-compliance
Lightning Source LLC
Chambersburg PA
CBHW031208270326
41931CB00006B/468